A Foray into the M

Everybody Hurts

Richard Bradbury

PNEUMA SPRINGS PUBLISHING UK

First Published in 2017 by:
Pneuma Springs Publishing

Everybody Hurts
Copyright © 2017   Richard Bradbury
ISBN13: 9781782284406

Richard Bradbury has asserted his right under the Copyright, Designs and
Patents Act, 1988, to be identified as Author of this Work

British Library Cataloguing in Publication Data. A catalogue record for
this book is available from the British Library.

Cover artwork: painted by Michelangelo and his assistants for the Sistine
Chapel in the Vatican between 1508 to 1512. Public domain artwork.

Pneuma Springs Publishing
A Subsidiary of Pneuma Springs Ltd.
7 Groveherst Road, Dartford Kent, DA1 5JD.
E: admin@pneumasprings.co.uk
W: www.pneumasprings.co.uk

This books is dedicated to:

my wife, Carolyn,

my children, Katie, Emma, Joshua and Jonty, and

my grandchildren,

the support of all of whom keep me going at all times through all that life throws up.

Contents

Foreword

In some regards, it is unfortunate that the biblical books being considered here have been labelled as 'The Minor Prophets.' Their prophetic messages, both at the time they were given, and also today, are anything but minor. It would be true to say, however, that apart from the occasional stand out verse that we all use, their message has been largely misunderstand or misinterpreted.

This is where my friend Richard Bradbury's book comes into its own. In an accessible style that everyone will find engaging, Richard has clearly explained the context of the prophet's own life and the cultural and historical context of the prophet's message. Building on the clear and strong foundation of context, this book then allows us to see how those messages are not simply relevant as 2000 year-old history, but as the very word that God would speak to us today.

I love Richard's approach to this material, uncovering the 'nub', as he calls it, of the prophet's message and applying it to our lives today. Books like this are necessary in every generation so that the timeless messages given by these prophets can speak as the word of God for all of the people at all times.

I thoroughly endorse his approach and I highly recommend this book. It is a resource that deserves to be widely read.

A book about prophets and their writings, I guess, would not be fulfilling its purpose if that book itself were not prophetic. I'm glad to say, I found this book clearly carried a prophetic message for today which I know will be used by God to speak to you the reader.

Paul Benger
Lead Pastor, Christian Life Church

Introduction

There are many scholarly works abroad which consider the Minor Prophets in their historical context and in terms of their prophetic content. My aim in writing this book is not simply to repeat what has been written elsewhere, but rather to identify the nub of the message of each prophet and apply it in our post-modern, western setting.

This may not be an easy task and I hope to avoid platitudes and anachronism. However, if the word of God is the Word of God for all people at all times, then we need, not only to understand what it meant when it was written, but also what it means for us now. Without application, it can become just so much additional knowledge to furnish our brains. With application, it can change our life.

The Minor Prophets are not just a bunch of dead guys from over two millennia ago. They were men, raised up by God, to speak to nations. They were from all different backgrounds and walks of life – some were royalty, others were shepherds; some prophesied in wonderful poetic language whilst others spoke out of the basic things around them as they went about their daily lives. All of them, however, spoke the Word of the Lord into a live and real situation. Often it took courage to deliver that word and some paid for such bravery with their lives.

The record we have of their words in the Bible is both time-specific and universal. Some of their words have already been fulfilled but some, particularly the eschatological passages, are still to be fulfilled even in our day. Of course, we have the benefit of hindsight, and so much of the prophetic foreshortening that hampered many at the time of Jesus from being able to differentiate between those passages that spoke of his first coming and his Second Coming, can be avoided. However, we can never be complacent or assume too much when interpreting those passages that speak of things still future. This is the challenge facing any interpreter and so, in this work, I have chosen to focus on the present, without ignoring future implications, whilst not making too many hard and fast declarations about what is still to come.

Essentially, in this book, I will endeavour to focus on the oracles of a specific prophet per chapter, taking them in the order in which they appear in the Bible, essentially this is going to be a summary of each book with an application in each case.

For each book I will attempt to establish the following:

- Who the prophet was
- To whom was he prophesying
- When was he prophesying
- What was the political / religious situation into which he was prophesying
- What was the main message he wanted to convey
- What we can learn from this

I hope that, as a result of this approach, this book will be both readable, and will appeal to a wider audience than a more academic work. As you read it, I would encourage you to pray, asking God to help you apply the lessons within it to your own life.

Finally, once more, I have picked one of REM's songs as the title of this book. The role of a prophet was rarely a popular one in Old Testament times, and often led to rejection, persecution and death. Thus, I have entitled this book 'Everybody Hurts'. This is true for both the prophet and his audience in turn. Serving God is not always easy. It may be accompanied by difficulty and pain, but it reaps an eternal reward.

Hosea

Introduction

It was a time of peace in the country and in the region. Sure, there were conflicts elsewhere, but, in this particular region, there were none. This had a positive effect on the economy following a period of recession, and this in turn created a general sense of wellbeing amongst the people, particularly the more wealthy residents of the land.

Society, however, had become divided between the 'haves' and the 'have nots'. Many enjoyed the consumer lifestyle with its luxury goods. The height of fashion was to have a second home or 'summerhouse' to which you would go in the heat of the summer, usually in the hills. A new aristocracy had developed - the 'get rich quick' boys. But housing had become a problem because, as the rich got richer, the poor got poorer. The rich had second homes but many people didn't have one at all.

Morally, the effects of this affluence were very clear. There were financial scandals, bribery and corruption was rife and even the judiciary could not be trusted. There was no justice in the courts without the payment of backhanders to the judges. Traders were soon into seven-days-a-week trading because they could make more money that way. Avarice led to injustice and affluence led to permissiveness. Sexual laxity was the order of the day and alcohol consumption rose sharply.

I am not here describing Britain in the 21st Century but Israel 2,800 years ago at the time when Hosea was prophesying - around 720BC. In addition to the above, the people had gone away from the worship of God and had pursued the worship of the Baals and other idols. Such worship included unwholesome practices, including sleeping with temple prostitutes, to guarantee a good harvest for your crops, and these practices even included human sacrifice, usually of children.

Into this situation, God raised up a man named Hosea. He was called primarily to the Northern kingdom of Israel, although some of the prophecies in his book are also addressed to Judah. Hosea was God's last prophet to Israel before they were taken into exile by the Assyrians, but even at this late stage, God gave them every opportunity to repent and avoid the disaster that was coming upon them. The message fell on deaf ears and the people of Israel were exiled in 711BC.

Hosea himself was an urban northerner who prophesied about 10 years after Amos. His message was ignored by the nation and even mocked. However, the most powerful thing about this book is that Hosea was not just commissioned to proclaim the message God had given him, but to live it out. He became God's message to God's people.

Hosea 1:1-11, 3:1-5

In this first part of the book of Hosea we see the prophet, in his marriage to a prostitute, modelling God's love for unfaithful Israel. For someone such as Hosea, the idea of marrying a prostitute would have been shocking, especially for a prophet. The mismatched couple had three children, at least one of whom was not Hosea's, after which his wife returned to her former occupation.

The first child was named Jezreel reminding Israel of the slaughter that had taken place at Jezreel which merited the discipline of the Lord. This was the slaughter by Jehu of Ahab's seventy sons, and God promises through Hosea to avenge their blood (1:4).

The second child, a girl, was named Lo-Ruhamah, which means 'not loved' or 'not pitied'. This was a deprived child who did not have the love of her mother and reminded Israel of its unconcern about the injustice to the poor within its land.

The third child was a boy named Lo-Ammi which means 'not my people'. He was the child that was not Hosea's and so was disowned by his father. This was a reminder to Israel that God would disown them by allowing them to go into exile if they did not repent.

In chapter 3, we see the faithfulness of Hosea in spite of his wife's unfaithfulness. He accepts her back as his wife. He puts her under discipline. He brings her home but does not share his bed with her. This was to represent the discipline of exile that God was going to put Israel through. The result would ultimately be a return of the nation to God.

The remainder of the book contains the oracles of Hosea that give more detailed prophetic insight into the unfaithfulness of the nation, laying the blame for this squarely at the door of the priests, the prophets, princes and the profiteers. The priests should have taught the people the laws of God. The prophets had given false prophesies telling the people that God would not bring judgement on them when, according to Hosea, this was part of God's plan. The princes had overseen the lapse into immorality and corruption. The profiteers had exploited the poor. And yet underlying these oracles we see the heart of God crying out to his people, for example, 11:1-4.

When Israel was a child, I loved him,
and out of Egypt I called my son.

But the more they were called,
the more they went away from me.

They sacrificed to the Baals
and they burned incense to images.

It was I who taught Ephraim to walk,
taking them by the arms;
but they did not realize
it was I who healed them.

I led them with cords of human kindness,
with ties of love.

To them I was like one who lifts
a little child to the cheek,
and I bent down to feed them."

Despite the prophecy of impending judgement, there is also the promise of restoration (see especially chapter 14). Thus, God demonstrates his faithfulness to unfaithful Israel. It is he who will restore her. It is he who will take her to himself again. In this book, more than in any other, we can feel the heart of God towards Israel, His chosen ones. It is not a book centred around judgment, but instead reveals the love of God for his unfaithful people.

This prophecy of restoration was partly fulfilled at the post-exilic return to the land, but will be completely fulfilled in the End Times when Jesus returns.

Application

So, what does all this have to do with us in 21st Century Britain? I want to apply it on two levels: concerning the nation and concerning the church.

The Nation

The nation of Israel was in a covenant relationship with God. That is, they were in a relationship where they had committed themselves to be obedient to God's Law, and God had committed himself to bless them, protect them and enrich them. There were both blessings and curses associated with obedience or disobedience respectively. As we encounter them in Hosea, they were about to experience the curses of disobedience, as promised in Deuteronomy 27.

As a nation, we have never been covenanted to God in this way. We are not a 'Christian nation' - there is no such thing. In the new covenant, there is a complete separation between church and state despite what Constantine, the Popes, Henry the VIII or anyone else has tried to create otherwise. Our Laws may have been influenced by Judeo-Christian ethics, and we may, in the past, have had many godly men and women in positions of authority, but as a nation we could never have been said to have been totally Christian – Christianised maybe, but not Christian.

Right now, we are at the culmination of a process that has been in operation for about 150 years of the secularisation of our nation. Recent legislation is the fruit of that process and is an indicator of how far we have come.

We know from scripture that 'Righteousness exalts a nation, but sin condemns any people' (Proverbs 14:34). At one time God used this nation to take the gospel to the four corners of the world and we still have left some of the residue of that influence, but we live in days when the Christian influence that affected the whole world is now waning in our own backyard.

So, given the state of our nation, what can we expect in the future? In Matthew 25:34-36 Jesus gives us the Parable of the Sheep and the Goats which is an indicator of the judgement of the nations at his return. There are three ways that the reference to his 'brothers' can be interpreted (to mean Israel, the Church, or the poor of the world), but taken in its simplest form, it is an indicator that those nations who ignore, suppress, and deal unjustly with those who are poor, infirmed and in need will receive the judgement of God upon them at that time. I am not just talking about our own poor and needy, but those of the world to whom daily we turn a blind eye. In comparison with the poor of the developing world, the poorest in this country are wealthy, and yet we often ignore both.

The message of Hosea was a call to Israel to repent and become faithful to the God who had brought them out of bondage in Egypt. The only hope for our nation is that we, too, repent and act in righteousness. That we lay aside the gods of avarice, lasciviousness and selfishness, and renew our faith in the God who can save us, bless us and exalt us, acting in righteousness towards the poor and oppressed of the world, and making known the good news of the Kingdom as we once did.

We need to pray that our nation will rediscover her faith in God.

The Church

The call of Hosea to Israel addressed their unfaithfulness, but also emphasised God's faithfulness towards them as a people. Whilst our nation may not be covenanted to God, the church certainly is. That is what the New Covenant is all about. This means there is an expectation on us that, if the church wants to live under the blessing of God, it must also walk in obedience to God. This is not about re-establishing the Law, but rather of allowing God's Spirit to lead us into the fullness of the fruit of the Spirit in our lives.

If we look at the history of the church, it has been no more faithful in many ways than Israel. It has allowed power, wealth and corruption to dominate it. It has suppressed and persecuted people. It has not always demonstrated the holiness of God. Even now, the divisions of the church are an eyesore and a blot on the world's landscape.

We are called to be a 'Holy Nation' and that means, a people separated for God's own purposes. Our lives, individually and collectively, should exemplify the life of the Kingdom. We are called to be Jesus to the world. That may seem like a tall order, but how else will the world see and know who Jesus is except through us?

It is time for the bride to put on her white dress once more to prepare for the coming of the bridegroom. It is time for the church to become all that was in the heart of Jesus when he 'loved her and gave himself up for her to make her Holy' (Ephesians 5:25-26). When Jesus comes back to earth it will be for a perfect bride. It might take persecution and refining to produce that purified bride but so be it. We need to be a bride fit for a king.

Just as God was faithful to faithless Israel, so Jesus is faithful to his church. He has not and will not give up on us because he has invested his kingdom in us. But as the master in the parable of the talents in Matthew 25: 14-30 expected a return on the investment he had made in his servants, so Jesus also expects a return on the investment he has made in us.

Conclusion

God is faithful. He expects faithfulness from us. That means our whole hearts need to be given over to him and his purposes. Do we have adulterous hearts or are we totally given over to him?

Joel

Introduction

We do not know exactly when the prophet Joel was prophesying as there are no clear indicators in the text. Also, we have no identifiers as to who Joel was except that his name means 'Yahweh is God' and that his father's name, 'Pethuel', means 'the straightforwardness or sincerity of God'.

What is clear is that he believed he had the word of the Lord for Judah, and he proclaimed it to priests, elders, drunkards and farmers; in fact, to everyone and anyone who was willing to listen. This word had to do with the judgement that had come upon the land and it had a warning of further judgement to come. It included a call to repent, but in the midst of promises of judgement, the book of Joel is filled with hope.

Essentially, the book splits into three parts. The first part (1:1 – 2:17) is about the immediate situation of Israel at the time the prophecy was given. The second part (2:18-30) has to do with the 'Last Days' which began at Pentecost. The third part (2:31 – 3:21) concerns the coming kingdom. Thus, there is an emphasis on the past, the present and the future in this book.

We will consider each of these parts as we go through this brief study.

Past

The context of these prophecies is a massive and unusual locust invasion of the lands of Judah and Israel that has left the crops devastated. Such is the devastation that Joel begins by asking; 'Has anything like this ever happened in your days or in the days of your ancestors?' (1.2). In 1:4, Joel mentions different kinds of locusts all of which have contributed to the disaster.

'Apparently the swarming locust is none other than an ordinary species of grasshopper. When moisture and temperature conditions favour a large hatch, the crowding and unceasing contact and jostling of the nymphs stimulate significant changes, so that the grasshopper nymphs make a transition from solitary behaviour to the swarming, gregarious and migratory phases of the dreaded plague. Plagues continue as long as climactic conditions favour large hatches.

'Such swarms can cover great distances (they have been seen 1,200 miles out to sea), and can be of immense size (an area of 2,000 square miles was recorded around the Red Sea in 1881) and can contain huge numbers in tight density (up to 120 million per square mile). One female grasshopper, which lays her eggs in June, may have 18 million descendants in October. Swarming hordes often block out the sun, riding high on the wind. A swarm can contain up to 10 billion insects... The noise of locusts in a swarm has been likened to that of a jet engine, due to the twofold sound of whirring wings and crunching jaws...They can get into houses, even through cracks and chimneys. Pliny claims that they can even gnaw through doors. They strip the bark off trees. When dead, they give off a revolting stench, and their bodies breed typhus and other diseases in both animals and humans.'[1]

This locust invasion was a major disaster in Israel which devastated the vine, figs, barley and every other kind of crop in the land. Joel flags it up as a sign of God's judgement against Judah and he calls the nation to repentance. He tells the drunkards to 'wake up and weep' (1:5). He tells the farmers to respond with wailing (v.11). He tells the priests to 'put on sackcloth and mourn' (1:13). He summons elders to come and 'cry out to the Lord' (1:14). Such is the loss of grain and wine that the priests do not even have enough to make an offering to the Lord.

---

[1] David Prior, *The message of Joel, Micah & Habakkuk*, (Leicester: IVP, 1988), pp.18-19

The real issue is not just the devastation, but the response of the people to God. It has not driven them to set their hearts right before him and to seek him. What will it take to make a nation turn to seek God?

In my hearing, it is God who gets the blame when things go wrong – when natural disasters strike, when the harvest fails, when things go belly up. Instead of seeking the very one who can help, people blame him and dive further into their selfish living. Hedonism is an escape from the realities of a corrupt and fallen world in which nothing really makes sense and in which there appears to be no ultimate answers – or at least none that people want to hear. The pursuit of pleasure is 'the opiate of the masses,' to paraphrase Marx.

Having given them this warning, Joel tells them that, if they do not repent, there will be more to come (2:1-18). He says that the next horde that is coming is not locusts. Rather it is an invading army that will have the same devastating effect on the land as locusts. This was fulfilled when Babylon invaded in 605BC. They operated a scorched earth policy in which they killed off most of the inhabitants of the land, and devastated the crops so that nobody could reside there.

And yet, even in the midst of this prophecy of judgement, hope is extended. Joel says that all they have to do is return to the Lord and he will preserve and protect them (2:12-14). He goes on to suggest that it is fasting and intercession by the priests and the elders of the land that will save the people (2:15-17). The assurance for their prayers being heard is the compassion of God, who is 'slow to anger and abounding in love' (2:13). This is so important to remember. Our God is a good God. When we rebel against him, we take ourselves outside of his protection, but when we return to him, he responds in immeasurable grace and compassion. He receives us back, wraps his arms around us, and blesses us beyond all that we deserve.

There then follows the promise of abundance in the land and a call to rejoice in the goodness of God (2:18-27).

Present

Now we come to the section that deals with the present. I want to pick this up in two parts: restoration and outpouring.

The promise of restoration

In 2:25, Joel declares the word of God that he will 'restore the years the locusts have eaten'. Whilst this is a word specifically for Israel regarding the locust plague that had just passed through them, and the subsequent dearth in the years during which they recovered from this plague, there is also a spiritual principle here. It is the fact that God is a God of restoration.

Many of us go through difficult periods in our lives. It might seem that we go through times of barrenness when nothing we put our hand to becomes fruitful. It may be that we go through a time of physical or emotional hardship when we wonder what God is doing and why it is happening to us. It may be that we go through a time of rebellion when we waste years away from God pursuing our own interests.

Whatever is the source of our fruitlessness, God is a God of restoration. Just as he promised to restore to Israel everything that was lost to them because of the plague of locusts, so he will restore to us everything we have lost as a result of the devastation that has come upon our lives. The Lord says, 'the time of barrenness is over; the time of fruitfulness is coming upon you'.

It may be that you will need to repent and seek him afresh. It may be that you will need to lay aside bitterness and unforgiveness. It may be that you will need to allow him back into your heart. Whatever it takes, do it, because the promise of restoration is there for the taking, and God would hold out his hand to you even today to restore all that has been lost.

The promise of the Spirit

In 2:28-32, we have the promise of the Spirit that was fulfilled on the Day of Pentecost. It was these words that Peter quoted as he stood before the crowds preaching his first post-resurrection sermon. There are a number of factors in this:

1. God wants to pour out his Spirit on everyone. Nobody is excluded from this. If you have not experienced the outpouring of the Spirit of God, today is your day. God wants us all to be filled to overflowing with his Spirit. The Spirit is to be a well of water springing up to eternal life from within us, and flowing out from us to touch and refresh those around us. Don't be content with half-measures. Seek God again for the river to flow in abundance from within.

2. This outpouring is not limited according to gender, race or social position. It is for everybody. Do not think you are not good enough. God wants to release his abundance in you and through you.

3. The result will be supernatural revelation: prophecy, dreams and visions. I believe that God wants to release more of the prophetic amongst his people. It does not matter how young you are or how old you are – you can dream dreams or see visions. It does not matter whether you are male or female – you can prophesy. As we seek God, so he will release the prophetic amongst us in abundance.

As a result of this outpouring, God wants to see people calling on his name to be saved and delivered (2:32). The onus is on each one of us to seek him so that he might release the prophetic amongst us and so that we may be able to build up, encourage and exhort one another in order to complete the work he has given us to do on earth. Seek him today for revelation and I am sure you will not be disappointed.

Future

In 2:31, we have an indicator of some cosmic events in the sky above which are portents of the Day of the Lord – the Second Coming of Christ. In Matthew 24:29, Jesus quotes these verses and tells us that they will be **the** sign of his coming. This leads us onto the last section of this book (Chapter 3), which has to do with the end times. Again, there are two elements to this: judgement and blessing.

The first part of the chapter (3:1-15) is about the judgement of the nations that will occur during the End Times. We are given a number of details about this judgement in 3:2:

- It is a gathering of all nations.
- It will take place in the valley of Jehoshaphat. This valley is near Tekoa which is where Amos came from, and is 11 miles south of Jerusalem. It was the valley in which Jehoshaphat defeated the combined armies of Moab, Ammon and Edom in 2 Chronicles 20 when he called the nation to repentance and prayer and, in response to the revelation of God, sent the singers out in front of the army to praise. It is thus a place of historic victory for Israel.
- The basis of this judgement is how the nations have treated Israel.

This judgement on the nations is portrayed symbolically and we are not sure exactly how God will carry it out, but it will not be pleasant for those gathered there.

The second part of this chapter refers to the end time blessing that will come upon the land following this judgement and at the Lord's return. It contains once more the eternal promise of restoration to the land for Israel (3:20). It also has the same reference as is found in Amos about the mountains 'dripping with new wine'. In other words, the undoing of the Eden curse will result in the earth bringing forth an abundance for all to enjoy. This is what we will experience in the millennial kingdom of Christ when creation is restored in full (see Romans 8:18-22). At that time, the earth will be like the original Eden, bringing forth an abundance for all to enjoy. The earth will be in equilibrium under the headship of Jesus Christ and the original intention for the earth will reach its fulfilment.

Conclusion

The book ends with the phrase 'The Lord dwells in Zion'. Of course, 'Zion' is the name of the hill on which the temple stood. When the Lord returns, he will rule from that same point, but at the present time, the temple of the living God is his church.

Right now, the Lord dwells here amongst us. We are his dwelling place. It is here that the presence of God can be felt. It is in our corporeity that the Lord is revealed. Whilst my body is a temple, the temple reaches its fulfilment in our worship together. When we come together to worship, with all else laid aside, the Spirit of God comes amongst us and makes us his dwelling place.

Who knows, as we move forward, that the presence of God will be so evident amongst us that we cannot even stand to minister. Our churches should be places where the glory of the Lord will be seen. May it be so!

Amos

Introduction

In this book, we encounter a man who is the last person you would expect to be called as a prophet. There are many things that humanly speaking would disqualify him from such a role.

Firstly, he was just a poor farmer. He was from a place called Tekoa which is 12 miles south of Jerusalem. It is described as being next to the wilderness so was not exactly the best place for farming or sheep rearing. He also looked after sycamore trees (7:14). Such employment was regarded as one of the lowest jobs because the sycamore figs were the food of the poorest people in the land. He was the complete opposite of the urbane Hosea whom we looked at previously. Who would listen to an unsophisticated yokel farmer who thought he had a message from God?

Secondly, he had no religious training; he was not a member of a priestly family; he had no education. He was a man quite simply called and anointed by God for a prophetic ministry. Smith Wigglesworth springs to mind.

Thirdly, Amos was a poor southerner whom God sent to preach to northerners. This is someone I can relate to! People are not always well received when they go out of their own people group. Amos was just a southern softy going to the northern rebels. Added to this, Israel and Judah had been at war on and off for about 200 years. When Amos arrived, he did not come to encourage them, but rather to bring God's judgement upon them – a popular message I am sure.

Despite all of this, under God's hand and by God's grace he was just the right man to bring this message to Israel.

Summary of the Book

Amos arrives at Bethel at the beginning of the book and begins to give the oracles that God has given to him. He describes them by saying 'the Lord roars from Zion' (1:2). Thus, he is saying that God is like a lion roaring so watch out! Having delivered his oracles, he picks up this same theme in 3:2-8 concluding 'the lion has roared...the Sovereign Lord has spoken'. The significance of this is that the Lord was seen as the shepherd of Israel - the one who would protect the flock from the lions who would prey on the sheep. Instead, the Lord is presented as the lion who would bring judgement upon them, and, in 3:12, the remnant that will be left is likened to 'two leg bones or a piece of ear' rescued from the lion's mouth.

He begins his oracles in chapter 1 by proclaiming judgement against Damascus, Tyre and Gaza – all non-Israeli cities. At this point his audience are listening with big smiles on their faces. Their expectation is that the Day of the Lord will be accompanied by judgement on the surrounding nations who have given them grief over the years. Next, he turns to Israel's cousins: Ammon, Moab and Edom. The smile on the face of his audience grows a little wider. Then he condemns their sister nation, Judah. By now the smile is a wide grin. But then he turns on them.

Picking up on what we said previously about the situation into which both Amos and Hosea were prophesying, the northern kingdom had been going through a time of affluence during which the rich were getting richer but were doing so by exploiting the poor of the land (2:6-8).

This is what the Lord says:
"For three sins of Israel, even for four, I will not relent.
They sell the innocent for silver, and the needy for a pair of sandals.

*They trample on the heads of the poor as on the dust of the ground
and deny justice to the oppressed.
Father and son use the same girl and so profane my holy name.
They lie down beside every altar on garments taken in pledge.
In the house of their god they drink wine taken as fines.*

Amos proclaims that their indifference toward, and exploitation of the poor, their moral laxity, and their disregard for the privilege of being the chosen people of God (3:2), will result in the loss of their wealth, fine furniture and second houses, and their exile from the land (3:11-15).

In chapters 4-6, Amos repeats and expands on many of these themes with respect to their treatment of the poor, even accusing them of taxing the straw and the grain of the poor so that they can build their mansions (5:11), and he confirms the judgements that would follow.

In chapter seven, we see the power of the prayers of a righteous man. God reveals to Amos two potential judgements that he will bring on Israel and each time, in response to Amos's plea, God tells him that these judgements will not happen. Instead, the Lord tells him that a plumb line will be held up against the nation, and judgement will be made against that plumb line.

But then, in the middle of this chapter we have an autobiographical section – the only one in the book (7:10-16). Amaziah, the priest of Bethel, tells him to stop prophesying. In response, he reiterates his call and carries on prophesying. How will we react when this world tells us to stop preaching the gospel? Don't tell me it won't happen here.

Just in the recent past, Victoria Wasteney was suspended because she was sharing her faith with a Muslim colleague in the health service. She shared as friends, invited her to Christian meetings, lent her a book about the conversion of a

Muslim woman to Christianity, offered to pray for her for some specific issues, all in the context of friendship and sharing about their respective faiths. The Muslim colleague eventually submitted a complaint and the Christian was suspended and her appeal dismissed. What is at stake here is our freedom to share our faith with others. Many of us may have done the same in the work place. I fear our freedom to do so in the future will be curtailed. How will you react?

Amos carried on prophesying despite the strictures put on him to stop.

The real issue for Amos was that the people he was preaching to were complacent and comfortable. The economy was doing well, there was peace on their borders, the religion established by Jeroboam two centuries before centred on Bethel and Dan was still going and was giving the people a focal point for their religious life (even though it was concentrated on two golden calves). Surely, in all these ways God was blessing them and they had no real need to repent. The hints that had been given to them in terms of occasional famines, plagues and a massive earthquake were all ignored by them as being signs of impending judgement as they were still comfortable and at peace.

Complacency kills faith. When we are comfortable and at peace, we have no perceived need of God. When people are comfortable in their lives, that is when they start to grow cold. Listen, financial prosperity, career advancement, relational stability are not the signs of God's blessing. God may bless us in these ways, but they can also be a stumbling block to us fulfilling the purpose of God in our lives. We can get so caught up with our career that we neglect our calling. We can get so comfortable with our material goods that we are not ready to go when God says go. We can get so caught up in our relationships that we become dependent on them instead of God.

We are called to discipleship. We are called to the narrow gate – the path less trodden. Christianity is not about coming to a set of beliefs, but is about a change in ownership. I am no longer in control of my life, God is. I must submit my will and all that I have to him. It is only then that I will find my true destiny and be all that I am called to be. It is only then that I will truly please my Father in heaven.

David's Fallen Tent

The book of Amos ends on a very positive note. I want to focus on this part in the remainder of this chapter (9:11-15).

It starts with 'in that day'. This is a reference to the Day of the Lord – the expected arrival of the Messiah. This is referred to in all of the prophetic books. Amos gives us some specific things to expect when the Day of the Lord came / comes. This also highlights that, for us, the Day of the Lord has already come, and yet is still to come. In this, we encounter 'prophetic foreshortening,' where events associated with the first and Second Coming of Jesus appear together in the same Old Testament passages. With the benefit of hindsight and with the help of the Holy Spirit, we can disentangle these events in order to see where scriptural prophecy has already been fulfilled and where it is still yet to be fulfilled.

The section begins with a reference to David's fallen tent. To what does this refer? We first encounter this tent in 1 Chronicles 16:1-6. It was not like the Tabernacle created in the Wilderness by Moses, or the Temple that would later be built by Solomon. It was a place where, in the presence of God, represented by the Ark, people were appointed to do nothing but sing songs and worship God. 16:39ff tells us that the Tabernacle was still at Gibeon and the sacrifices were still to take place there, but that here worship was the order of the day. This was an open tent – a place where all could come and join in with the worship of God. In the tabernacle or Temple, worship was centred on sacrifice, but here, worship was centred on a corporate response to the presence of God.

This tent is symbolic of New Covenant worship, compared to the Old Covenant worship that was still happening at Gibeon. James picks up on this in Acts 15:16 where he quotes Amos 9:11-12 and says that the New Covenant is open for all people from every nation to come and worship in the presence of the Lord without the need to come by way of fulfilment of the Law. Why? Because Jesus has fulfilled the law on our behalf. The way has now been opened up through grace. We are now 'fellow heirs, members of the same body and partakers of the promise in Christ Jesus, through the gospel' (Ephesians 3:6).

It is our privilege to come, not before the Ark, but into the presence of God as we gather together each Sunday. In doing so, we join with Asaph and the other people David appointed to stand before the Ark of the Lord to sing our songs and proclaim 'the excellencies of him who called us out of darkness into his marvellous light' (1 Peter 2:9). This is what New Covenant worship is all about. It is not about dead ritual but live and energetic worship that lifts the name of Jesus high, that exalts Yahweh, and that makes known his greatness and his mighty deeds. This is the fulfilment of the promise given through Amos.

When we come into the house of God, which is not the building but the gathered people of God, we do not come to sit and mope, sing a few songs and go home unchanged. We come to encounter the living God! And as we enter into worship, giving our all to him, so we will do so and he will lift us, encourage us, bless us and move us on in himself. Embrace the privilege of worship that is ours in the New Covenant.

The reaper will be overtaken by the ploughman

Then we come to 9:13-15.

These are verses full of the promise of restoration to the land for Israel. However, they are not just concerned with a return but also of the nation being blessed in the land, just as was promised in Deuteronomy 28. This was partially fulfilled in 535BC when they began to return to the land from exile, but the last part promises that they will never be removed from the land again (9:15). This is yet to be fulfilled as, after the sacking of Jerusalem in 70AD, and after the Bar Kochba revolt of 132AD, Israel was scattered once more.

In 1948, we saw the re-establishment of the state of Israel which was the beginning of seeing these verses fulfilled in totality. A day is coming, at the return of Jesus, when this will be fulfilled for literal Israel.

There is also a looking forward to the time when the curse that came upon the earth as a result of the Fall will be broken once and for all. It is as if the earth breaks forth in spontaneous abundance and fruitfulness. Wine will drip from the mountains and flow from the hills.

This whole section speaks of the future fruitfulness and peace that will come upon the earth under the Messiah's reign. Of course, we already have the spiritual blessings that come through the cross – forgiveness, restoration, access, relationship, and many more. But a day is coming when God will return this earth to the divine intention as Jesus reigns upon the earth and brings all things back in perfect order.

In the meantime, there have been and will be times of revival on this earth when the 'reaper is overtaken by the ploughman' – when people respond to the gospel faster than it can actually be preached. May we see that in our day. It is only a revival that will bring our nation back from the edge.

May we lay aside all that gets in the way of seeing that happen, and may we pray to see such an outpouring of the Spirit of God that we cannot keep up with the work as God brings many people into his kingdom.

Obadiah

Introduction

Obadiah is thought by most scholars to be the first of the Old Testament prophets whose prophesies have been captured in written form as distinct documents. He was prophesying around 845BC (although some suggest he may have been prophesying as late as 587BC). A stream of other prophets arose after him all calling the nation of Israel back to God as well as prophesying concerning the surrounding nations. At just 21 verses, this is also the shortest book in the Old Testament.

His name means 'worshipper or servant of God'. We know little else about him from the text – not even his father's name.

The prophecy has three themes:

1. Judgement against Edom
2. Judgement against the nations
3. Blessing for Israel.

We will consider these themes throughout the rest of this study.

Judgement against Edom

The relationship between Israel and Edom had always been a little fraught. It had its roots in the relationship between Jacob and Esau. You will remember in the story that these two were twins, but that Esau was born first with Jacob hanging on to his heel (Genesis 25:26). As they were growing up, Esau was favoured by his father (always a mistake!) and Jacob was a mummy's boy.

Esau, of course, had traded his birthright to Jacob for a pot of lentils and had thereby despised it. Nevertheless, when they came of age, and Isaac wanted to pass on his blessing to Esau, he was ready to go out hunting to bring some game for his father in order to gain the inheritance. Fortunately (or unfortunately) for Jacob, he had a trickster mother, Rebekah, who helped him to cheat his brother Esau out of the inheritance, after which Jacob fled for twenty years. When he returned, with flocks, two wives, two concubines and 11 children, there was some reconciliation between them, but they agreed to live in different parts of the land. Jacob stayed on the west bank of the Jordan and Esau went to the east bank.

The area where Esau settled was around Mount Seir – the southern part of modern Jordan. There were two major cities in Edom: Bosrah and Sela (known today as Petra). Much of this area is mountainous, hence, Petra is carved out of the rock. This is referred to in Obadiah (v.3). Effectively, the Edomites built mountain strongholds and, thus, made themselves secure (and proud – v.3).

The next time we encounter Edom is in Deuteronomy 2:1-7, when the people of Israel were travelling from the wilderness of Sinai towards the Promised Land to capture it. In these verses, they are told not to go through Edom because Edom is a related nation, and God was not planning to give Israel any of the territory he had allotted to them. The detail of this encounter, related in Numbers 20, informs us that the Edomites came out with an army against Israel to ensure they did not pass through their territory.

During the reign of David, when the kingdom of Israel reached its zenith, Edom became a satellite nation to Israel (2 Samuel 8:14). They remained so until the kingdom began to crumble. From the time of Jehoram (2 Kings 8:20), they were in rebellion against Judah (between 849 and 842 – around the time that Obadiah was prophesying). From this point on, whenever anyone attacked Judah, Edom would join in with them, and it is this that Obadiah is prophesying about (v.10).

Indeed, when Babylon overran Judah, Edom assisted them. They also betrayed to the Babylonians any Israelites who had fled, handing them over to the Babylonians for execution or slavery, and they also assisted the Babylonians in the looting of the city of Jerusalem. The heart of Obadiah's prophesy against Edom is that, in spite of the fact that they were brothers of Israel, they acted towards them like the worst of enemies (v.11-14). It is because of their actions towards the people of God that they have merited a future judgement that will lead to their future destruction and this, indeed, did occur in the centuries that followed.

Judgement against the nations

In verses 15-18 of this prophecy, Obadiah identifies the judgement of Edom as part of the judgement of the nations that would follow. This is on the basis of how they have treated the people of God (v.15). Just as Edom was being judged for its treatment of Israel, so the nations will be judged on the same basis.

In Matthew 25, Jesus picks up this same theme concerning the Judgement of the nations at His coming. This passage is not to do with judgement of the righteous and unrighteous per se. Rather, it is a specific judgement concerning how the nations have treated 'these brothers of mine'. We have three options concerning who these 'brothers' are:

- The physical brothers of Jesus, i.e. the Jews
- The spiritual brothers of Jesus, i.e. the Church
- Those whom Jesus identifies as brothers, i.e. the downtrodden (the hungry, thirsty, strangers, naked, sick, and imprisoned)

Of these options, the first accords most consistently with scripture (Joel 3:1-17, Zechariah 14:1-8, etc. and particularly

Obadiah). The judgement upon the nations is not simply for how they have treated (or mistreated) the Jews, but also for how they have neglected to care for them despite the dispersion.

Blessing for Israel

The last verses of the book (19-21), speak of the restoration of Israel to the land, and, as I have stated previously in this book, we have seen this taking place since the middle of the twentieth century.

Application

A key theme in this book is about one brother acting appropriately towards another brother. This is summed up in verse 12: 'You should not gloat over your brother in the day of his misfortune'. What is our attitude towards our brothers and sisters in Christ? Is it positive or negative? I am not just speaking about people in our own church, although that applies, but people in other churches. They may meet in a different place; they may not worship in the same way as we do; they may not see eye to eye with us theologically on a range of issues, but, if they are our brothers and sisters, we should maintain a positive attitude towards them.

Jesus, himself, taught us in John 13:35, "By this everyone will know that you are my disciples, if you love one another." It is our attitude towards one another that marks us out as disciples and which is a testimony to the world of who we are. Over the centuries, those in the church have been anything but loving towards one another. We have fallen out, separated and divided, fought and even burned one another at the stake. We have not covered ourselves in glory by these actions.

In our day, we have opportunities to join with churches from across the denominations. This is not about organisational unity, but about unity in the Spirit. Psalm 133 tells us clearly that where there is unity, there is blessing. Do not neglect the opportunity to fellowship with brothers and sisters even when it seems difficult and painful.

Coming back to our own individual situations, is there anyone in the local body with whom you are not in unity? Is there anyone with whom there is a relationship issue? Have you criticised them or spoken negatively about them to anyone else? It is time to get it sorted. The enemy is a 'roaring lion seeking someone to devour'. In other words, he is looking for anywhere he can get in between us to mar or destroy our relationships. He knows that our strength is in our unity but 'If a house is divided against itself, that house cannot stand' (Mark 3:25).

The enemy will look for every crack of upset or division in our relationships and will seek to exploit it in order to weaken us. We each have a choice: when someone or something upsets us, we can sit on it and let it fester, or we can deal with it through forgiveness and reconciliation. It may be that we can do that just between ourselves and God, or we may need to put something right with the individual or with the person we have gossiped to about that individual. Either way, we need to deal with these things.

The consequence of not dealing with relational issues in the body of Christ is that we weaken ourselves, we weaken the body, and we undermine our witness. We also become bitter and critical which is self-destructive. However, if we do deal with them, we strengthen the body.

Holding on to grudges and upsets, not dealing with issues, and remaining out of fellowship with another brother or sister are all contrary to kingdom behaviour. They are the ways of the world and not of the kingdom and we need to make a choice to separate ourselves from the ways of the world so that we can glorify Jesus.

Here are three illustrations of unity:

1. In a Peanuts cartoon Lucy demanded that Linus change TV channels, threatening him with her fist if he didn't. "What makes you think you can walk right in here and take over?" asks Linus.

   "These five fingers," says Lucy. "Individually they're nothing but when I curl them together like this into a single unit, they form a weapon that is terrible to behold."

   "Which channel do you want?" asks Linus. Turning away, he looks at his fingers and says, "Why can't you guys get organised like that?"

   When we are together, we are stronger than when we are apart. We are a weapon in the hand of God that can be used to do much damage against the enemy.

2. Snowflakes are one of nature's most fragile things, but just look at what they can do when they stick together. Once more, when we are together, even the weakest and most fragile of us can be part of that vast army that can cause havoc.

3. Tonto and the Lone Ranger were riding through a canyon together when all of a sudden both sides were filled with Native American warriors on horses, dressed for battle. The Lone Ranger turned to Tonto and asked, "What are we going to do?" Tonto replied, "What's with this 'we' paleface?". When the rubber hits the road, are we really united with this body or ready to turn away to save ourselves?

Conclusion

The message of Obadiah is that brothers should treat each other as brothers. We too, have a responsibility to do the same in the Body of Christ. I appeal to you as a fellow brother, be united with one another. Sort out any differences and let us move on in the strength that the Lord provides.

Jonah

Introduction

The book of Jonah is distinct from the other Minor Prophets in that it is not a set of oracles but rather is a narrative concerning the prophet himself. It tells the story of his call to go to Nineveh and the events that followed. There are no prophetic oracles in this story, so why is it amongst the prophetic books? Because God is saying something very important through it as we shall see.

We are told in 1:1 that Jonah was the son of Amittai. We know from 2 Kings 14:25 that he was from Gath Hepher which was a small hilltop village about 5kms north of Nazareth and 1km from Cana. We also know that Jonah was prophesying during the reign of Jeroboam II who reigned in the Northern Kingdom of Israel from Samaria. Jeroboam reigned for 41 years and is described in 2 Kings 14:24 as an evil king. Nevertheless, in accordance with the prophecies of Jonah, he recovered much land for Israel during his reign.

Thus, Jonah was prophesying around 770BC primarily in the Northern Kingdom of Israel. At this time, the dominant power of the region was Assyria and had been since 1354BC. They exercised Hegemony over the whole region and for a short period even ruled over Egypt. As such, they were the biggest threat and enemy to Israel and in 710BC took the Northern Kingdom of Israel into captivity. The capital of Assyria – the place where the king had his palace – was Nineveh, and so the command of the Lord to Jonah was to go to the centre of government for Israel's biggest enemy and tell them they were going to be destroyed by God if they did not repent from their wicked ways. For you and I this would be like going to Moscow and proclaiming destruction on Russia if they did not stop messing around in other sovereign states.

Make no bones about it, the Assyrian regime was an evil one. One of the favourite methods of dealing with enemies was to impale them on wooden spikes until they died, and they would do this to thousands of people at one time. It was a ruthless and cruel empire which dominated its subject nations by fear.

The narrative

So, what is Jonah's response when he is given this instruction? 'Of course I'll go to them Lord'. No rather, and not surprisingly perhaps, he runs in the opposite direction. Instead of travelling north and east, he travels south and west. He goes to Joppa (modern day Jaffa - part of Tel Aviv) and boards a boat bound for Tarshish. There is uncertainty concerning where exactly Tarshish was. It could be Carthage, Spain or even Sardinia. What is certain is that it was nowhere near Nineveh and was as far away from there as Jonah could get.

God said to Jonah simply 'Go to Nineveh and preach'. What has God asked you to do? When God asks us to do something that we may not be keen on what is our response? Is it to go immediately and do it or to run in the opposite direction? Only you know the answer to that question. Only you know what God has put in your heart and how you have responded. It may be a calling that he has placed upon your life that you have resisted. It may be quite simply a word that he has dropped in your heart to give to somebody else, or an act of kindness that he has asked you to carry out for someone you do not really know. How do we respond when he speaks to us?

Jonah had obeyed God previously when he was sent to the wicked king of Israel and had prophesied blessing over him (2 Kings 14:25). We will find out later in the book why he was reluctant to go to these wicked people. However, it is not for us to pick and choose the tasks God gives us to do. Our duty is simply to obey and trust him for the outcome.

God has a way of dealing with our disobedience that is not always pleasant. As it says in Hebrews 12:6, 'Those the Lord loves he disciplines'. In this case (1:4) he sent a 'violent wind' to create a storm so that the sailors were in fear of their lives. Where was Jonah while this was going on? Below deck asleep, blissfully unaware of the imminent threat to his life. It soon starts to unravel, however, when the captain wakes him up to tell him to pray to his God and then they cast lots to see who is responsible for the storm and the lot falls to Jonah.

When he told them to throw him overboard, do you think Jonah had any hope of survival? I think he had come to realise that his disobedience was responsible for this trouble and that, having disobeyed God, he believed he might as well end his life. I would not suggest that should be our response when we are in disobedience, however, Jonah knew he had seriously messed up.

The psalm of Jonah in chapter 2 of the book is an open and honest response to all that has gone on. The language he uses is of actual death – the seaweed wrapped around his head and he sank to the bottom of the sea (v.5). Also, he talks of being in 'the realm of the dead' (v.1). This of course may be poetic language to describe what happened to him or it may be that he did actually die and was resurrected after the fish spat him out on dry land. If this is the case, how much more is he representative of Jesus – it is the Lord himself who cites Jonah as an example of what would happen to him:

"For as Jonah was three days and three nights in the belly of a huge fish, so the Son of Man will be three days and three nights in the heart of the earth" (Matthew 3:40).

Jonah, is a picture of resurrection. For us, he is also a picture of restoration. God never gave up on Jonah. Even when he had run away from God, even when he was falling beneath the waves of the sea, God still had a plan for his life.

Maybe you have said 'no' to God. Maybe you have run away from your destiny. Maybe you are still in that place, but God says to you, 'I have not given up on you'. Even though you may think you have lost all hope, or have put yourself beyond his use, he is still with you. His grace is extended to you and he will restore you and fulfil what he has spoken over your life.

When I was eighteen I ran away from God and his purposes for my life for a short time until, reluctantly, I gave in knowing that as far as I could run from God I could never get away from him. When I was thirty I disobeyed God, and suffered the consequences of that, but I am a living testimony of the fact that God is a God of restoration. It does not matter what you have done, or how bad you feel about it, if you will turn and repent before God, and make a choice to live in obedience to him, he will restore you; he will re-envision you; he will re-commission you. Our God is a God of second chances.

And here we see it in chapter 3:1, 'Then the word of the Lord came to Jonah a second time: 'Go to the great city of Nineveh and proclaim to it the message I give you''.

So, Jonah went and did exactly what he had been told to do. He preached from one end of the city to the other and sparked a bottom up revival that went all the way into the palace of the king. We are not sure which Assyrian king this was except that he reigned between Shalmanesser IV and V.

The response of the Assyrians to the preaching of Jonah was repentance. The response of God to the Assyrians was mercy – he postponed the promised judgement upon them – it didn't take place for another 150 years in response to Nahum's prophecies, as we shall see elsewhere in this book.

The reaction of Jonah was to sulk. What is our response when things don't work out as we hope?

Jonah actually wanted the judgement to be fulfilled. He even set himself up in a little camp outside the city to watch while it happened. He wanted to see the enemies of his people laid waste. He had reluctantly obeyed the Lord and now wanted to sit back and enjoy the show. However, he is not totally surprised when it doesn't happen.

From 4:1-3, we discover the real reason why Jonah was reluctant to set out from Galilee to preach to Nineveh. It wasn't about fear of the Assyrians. He had overcome fear when he had gone to the evil king of Israel. In fact, he'd already had a conversation with God about his reluctance to go whilst back home. He knew that God was merciful and would relent of carrying out his judgement given any glimmer of hope in the response of the Assyrians. Jonah knew his trip would not only be a waste of time, but that there was a high likelihood that the destruction he longed for to come upon Israel's enemies would not happen anyway. It is at this point he once more becomes suicidal. The whole trip for him – his travelling, his preaching, his prophesying - has been pointless from his perspective. "God, I knew you wouldn't carry out your threat if they repented so why did I bother?"

As we look at what is going on in the world, I am sure we can pick out peoples on whom we wish the judgement of God would fall and we ask why God allows them to continue. There are people in the workplace who do not act righteously and yet they always seem to get away with it and do not seem to get their comeuppance. We can end up getting angry at the apparent injustice of it all just like Jonah. And yet it is not God's delight to make anyone suffer.

Jonah seems to understand something of God's mercy towards people and his reluctance to treat them as their sins merit, but he does not understand the love and compassion of God. In order to demonstrate this, God gives him a plant for shelter and then allows it to be destroyed by a worm. Jonah is more upset about losing his shelter than that a hundred and twenty thousand people would be destroyed if God did not hold back his judgement in mercy and love.

We may understand the mercy of God, and have probably experienced it, but we also need to know the love and compassion of God. Mercy is an action but love is the motivation. God is motivated by love:

'For God so loved the world that he gave his only son that whoever believes in him shall not perish but will have everlasting life' (John 3:16).

It is the love of God that drove him to provide for us a means of salvation. It is the love of God that sent his son to this world to suffer and die for us in our place. It is the love of God that makes us 'children of God'. It is the love of God that draws us to himself. His mercy flows out of his undeserved love for us.

Some of us know a little of human love: we have experienced it and have given it. But all human love is ultimately selfish in that it is motivated by mutual benefit. God's love is truly altruistic in that it is poured out on the undeserving objects of his wrath, and results in their total and complete restoration to all that is truly human.

This whole book is not primarily about a big fish and a reluctant prophet. Rather it is the story of God's love visited on an undeserving people to save them from destruction and to bring them into relationship with himself. It is the same gospel that has reached out to us.

Conclusion

If you are running away from God, today is the day to turn back to him. You may not encounter a stormy sea or a big fish along the way, but God will always set out to draw you back to himself. Stop running! You can't get away. Just yield to him – it will make your life so much easier.

If, in the past, you have said no to God and feel shut out of his purposes as a result, know that God is a God of restoration. He wants to re-commission you and put you back on the road to fulfil your destiny.

If you would rather see the judgement of God and not mercy on those who do evil in the world, ask God to soften your heart so that you might see His creatures from His perspective. Yes, God does at times judge and will judge, but he always does so reluctantly, only when his love has not prevailed. Pray for them that they might come to realise the mercy and love of God and turn to him.

Micah

Introduction

Micah was prophesying at the same time as Isaiah and Hosea. Both of those prophets were prophesying in the city: Isaiah in Jerusalem and Hosea in Samaria. They were also both from wealthy backgrounds, Isaiah being from the royal family. In contrast with Isaiah, Micah was from the country and from a farming community. We are told in 1:1 that he was from Moresheth, a town between Jerusalem and the Gaza strip, the area occupied by the Philistines. It is clear from the prophesies that, in keeping with his background, Micah has a heart for the poor, ordinary people of the land who were being exploited.

These prophesies were given when 'Jotham, Ahaz and Hezekiah were kings of Judah' (1:1). This period begins around 750BC onwards and the prophecies seem to continue to just before the exile of the Northern kingdom under the Assyrians. Of these kings, Ahaz was evil - leading the people into the sins of the Northern Kingdom - Jotham was good but didn't deal with the nation's idolatry, and Hezekiah was very good, bringing the people back to the worship of Yahweh.

In his prophesies, Micah 'observed bribery amongst the judges, the prophets and the priests. The very people who should have upheld the law of God were being paid to say things that the people wanted to hear. There was exploitation of the powerless. Covetousness, greed, cheating, violence and cruelty became all too common. Crime was on the increase; landlords were stealing from the poor, evicting widows and orphans and putting them on the streets; merchants and traders were using inaccurate scales and weights so that business was corrupt. Sin was infiltrating every level of society. Above all, the rich and powerful were abusing the poor. Social and political power were being used to line pockets…Family relationships, the mainstay of any nation, were disintegrating. But Micah had a passion for social justice and has horrified that such things were happening among God's people – a people intended to be a light to the nations'.[2] As we've seen before, this could be a description of our modern world – there is nothing new under the sun.

In all of this, Micah was especially concerned with three problems: idolatry, immorality and injustice, and it was the last of these that was giving him the greatest alarm.

We can break the book up into three parts. Chapters 1-3 speak about crime and punishment – the bad things that are happening which God is going to deal with. As we have seen before, these things will bring the consequence of judgement and banishment on the nation. Chapters 4-5 focus on peace and security and the coming of the Messiah. Chapters 6-7 are about justice and mercy.

Chapters 1-3

In these chapters, Micah lists a number of place names and what will happen to them. What is lost in our English translation is that he uses the meaning of the names to describe their coming judgement. If he were living in East Yorkshire he might have said, 'Beverley will be overcome with beavers; Hull will be keelhauled; Driffield will drift off into a field; Goole will be invaded by Ghouls; Hornsea will be impaled upon a horn; Bridlington will be bridled like a horse'. The language construction of the prophecy is very clever in highlighting the sin and consequence of each of these towns. Within this, it is the influential leaders who are being held responsible for the situation. He points his finger at the king, the priests and the false prophets who had

---

[2]David Pawson, Unlocking the Bible: A Unique overview of the whole Bible (London: Harper Collins, 2007), p.527

allowed the spiritual decay to develop unhindered, but he was especially concerned with the profiteers (businessman & bankers) whose ruthless exploitation of the weak meant that the rich got richer and the poor got poorer.

Who should be held responsible for the state of our nation? Is it church leaders who have failed to take a stand or who have not spoken up for justice? Is it the philosophers and educationalists who have taken away the moral and ethical foundation of our country and replaced it with a relativistic soup where anything goes? Is it the politicians who have protected their own self-interest and lined their own nests for short-term gain? Is it the businessman and bankers who have put personal profit as their target regardless of the effect on people or on communities? Is it the pop stars who have educated the generations with a dialogue of self-indulgence and with an immoral example that has told successive generations that you can do what you like without reference to anyone else but yourself? 'I'm free to be whatever I choose, whatever I choose and I'll sing the blues if I want'.[3]

Perhaps we could think of a few more people to blame. All of these should have some share of the responsibility for the state of our nation, but so do we! If we have failed to speak out against injustice; if we have pursued selfish lifestyles at the expense of others; if we have not taken a stand against exploitation; if we have failed to live as righteous examples of godliness in a godless world, then we too share some of the responsibility for the state of our nation. My observation is that people are too quick to point the finger at others instead of looking into their own heart to see where the responsibility really lies. It is righteousness that exalts a nation (Proverbs 14:34). Let us look to our own righteousness, repent of our compromise, and seek to raise

---

[3] Oasis, Whatever, 1994

up a standard that will challenge the corruption of the society around us and raise once again a banner for the kingdom in this land.

Chapters 4-5

In chapters 4-5, we look forward to God ultimately sorting out the mess in this world and bringing in the kingdom. It includes references to the first coming of Christ (5:2-3 – often read at Christmas), but is mostly about the Second Coming when Jesus will bring in the kingdom in fullness.

We begin with 4:1-8. Vv.1-4 are identical to Isaiah 2:1-4. Which prophet wrote their version first is open to debate, but, suffice to say, the repeating of these prophetic phrases actually emphasises their validity and importance.

We see here the end time kingdom of peace being ruled from Jerusalem. It will be one in which there will no longer be a need for the weapons of war because these will be used for farming instead. It will be a time of direct rule by King Jesus from his political headquarters in Jerusalem over all the nations.

I just want to make one thing clear here, our ultimate destiny is not to sit on clouds in ethereal nightshirts plucking on harps in some otherworldly domain. Our destiny is to reign with Christ at his return. We will be part of the means through which this glorious administration will be exercised upon the earth. We are also not waiting for Jesus to come and snatch us out of the world before it capitulates in on itself. Rather, we are waiting for him to come and transform us into our eternal and perfect existence so that we will be fit to reign alongside him.

The work the Holy Spirit is doing in you right now is the preparation work of the 'not yet' kingdom. Your transformation from 'glory to glory' (1 Corinthians 3:18) is to get you ready to rule with Christ. Some of us are going to need a bit more work on that final day, but the challenge for us is to start living the values, the ethics and in the power of the kingdom now! That is how we will be ready for his coming.

Chapters 6-7

The last two chapters are a court scene. Just lately, my wife and I have begun to watch Judge Rinder. There are a number of things that do not cease to amaze us in watching this:

- The sad lives many people lead
- The ridiculous things people fall out over – especially families falling out over money
- The fairness and justice of the judge himself (in amongst all the showmanship) and his concern for people themselves

Anyone else who watches this will know that the setup is more like an American court than an English court. However, the notion of a court is what we see here in Micah, with the prophet himself playing the part of a defending barrister, and God himself as prosecuting counsel and judge.

The Lord argues that all his actions towards his people have been good (6:3-5) and yet the people have disdained him and turned away from him and from his laws. He declares, therefore, that the judgement against them that is already coming upon them is just. However, these chapters conclude in hope and confirmation that, despite the sin and judgement of the people, God will restore them and fulfil his promise to Abraham (7:20).

In the midst of these verses (6:6-8), Micah gives his response to the situation. He asks the question of himself as to what kind of sacrifice he could possibly make that will satisfy God and avert the disaster that is coming on the nation. He concludes that it is not sacrifice (or religious practice) that will save the nation, but rather a change of heart:

'To act justly, and to love mercy and to walk humbly with your God'

It is the injustice of the nation against the poor and oppressed that has merited the justice of God coming against them in judgement. But, just as God will once more show them mercy, so they must show mercy. It is humility before God that will keep justice and mercy in the right place.

A man was having his portrait painted and said to the artist, 'I hope this will do me justice.' The artist said, 'It is not justice you need, it is mercy!'

In this court scene, Micah is miserable when he considers the justice of God, but when he realises that God will also show mercy towards his people, his sorrow turns to rejoicing.

Sometimes we can consider God through his justice alone. We see him as a God of judgement and that he is. He will not tolerate sin, and especially the sin of injustice towards the poor. And yet in the midst of his judgement he always acts in mercy.

"But God commended his love towards us in that while we were still sinners Christ died for us' Romans 5:8.

There is nobody in this universe who needs to end up in hell. There is nobody for whom Jesus has not already borne the full punishment for their sins. There is nobody who needs to bear the guilt of sin. There is nobody who needs to continue in the trap of habitual sin. There is nobody who cannot be cleansed, renewed and set free from their past, present and future. It has all been achieved through the mercy of God poured out for us through the cross. Jesus has borne the judgement of God on our behalf so that we do not have to. There is no greater grace and mercy than that which flows from the Father's hand.

The image of an angry God does not do our Father justice. It needs to be replaced with the image of a God whose heart is broken at the destructive effects of sin on his beautiful creation and on his creatures, who has allowed his own son to become a substitute for us in order to redeem his creation and make it once more a heaven on earth. It is this that has been achieved on the cross, and it is this that will be seen once more on earth when Jesus comes to rule. That is the mercy of God poured out for us that should send us back to the Father in thanksgiving, praise, and in an outpouring of love for Him who in His justice remembered mercy.

Response

As we read the book of Micah there are three ways to respond:

Firstly, if we are not living as we should be (and we know it), we need to change. If we are living selfish self-centred lives without any regard for those around us, especially the poor and needy, we need to make choices to align ourselves with Jesus.

Secondly, we need to begin to live now in the light of the coming Kingdom of Peace. We can live now in righteousness and in trust in God our Saviour. We can begin to put things right in the world now, whether that be environmental mismanagement, injustice and poverty or slavery and oppression. There are things we can all do, not just in terms of our behaviour, but in terms of putting the world in God's order before Jesus comes to complete the task.

Thirdly, we can live our lives in the light of his mercy and seek to make that mercy known to others.

What does the Lord require of you? 'To act justly, and to love mercy and to walk humbly with your God'.

Nahum

Introduction

The name 'Nahum' means 'comfort'. There is not much comfort in the book for Nineveh, the city which Nahum was sent to prophesy against, however, this does bring comfort to Judah who had been oppressed by the Assyrians for many years. In order to understand this, we have to think back to the siege of Jerusalem by Sennacherib when Hezekiah was king, recorded in 2 Kings 18-19. The Assyrians had plundered and dominated the whole region for many years and, therefore, their destruction was to bring comfort to all of their enemies. What is bad news for the Assyrians is good news for all that have been oppressed by them.

Nahum is described in 1:1 as an 'Elkoshite'. It is not clear exactly which town this refers to, but it is probably Alkosh near Mosul in Northern Iraq. His tomb can be found there and is honoured by Arabs even to this day. This makes him one of the Northern Israelites taken into captivity by the Assyrians so it is not too surprising that he rejoices over their demise. Also, the town of Capernaum in Galilee was named after him. Capernaum means 'village of Nahum'.

Nahum lived at the same time as Zephaniah, Habakkuk and Jeremiah.

The Narrative

Like Jonah, Nahum was sent to Nineveh, however, his prophesies were given 150 years after Jonah's. Nineveh, of course, was the capital city of the major power of the world at the time, pending the supplanting of Assyria by Babylon. Jonah's message had been one of judgement to provoke repentance; Nahum's message proclaimed Nineveh's imminent destruction. There was no further opportunity for repentance in Nahum's message.

Following Jonah's oracles, Assyria had continued its expansion, taking over Egypt, and taking the 10 tribes of the Northern kingdom of Israel into captivity. Nahum, was prophesying not long before 612BC when Nineveh was actually destroyed, and he told them that their time had now run out.

150 years previously, in response to Jonah's prophecies, they had repented, but had soon slipped back into their cruel and barbarous ways. Despite the fact that God is slow to anger (v.3), their time was up and the judgement promised by both Jonah and Nahum (and Zephaniah) was about to come upon them. God tells them quite clearly in the last verse of this book, 'nothing can heal you', in other words 'there is no way out this time'.

In this book, there is also a sense of good news (see for example 1:15). There is the promise of restoration for Israel. Remember this is 5 years before the Babylonian captivity which saw the remaining part of the nation removed from the land. There is no mention of the exile within the prophecies of Nahum, but only the promise of national restoration at some stage.

The book splits into three parts, in accordance with the three chapters of the book. In the first part, we have the 'who': disaster for Assyria; deliverance for Israel and others. In the second part, we have the 'how', as Nahum describes the destruction that will come upon Assyria. In the third part, we have the 'why', as Nahum recalls the violence, cruelty, and witchcraft of the Assyrians that has led to their judgement.

Chapter 1 is an acrostic – that is each verse starts with a different letter from the Hebrew alphabet. It also alternates its thoughts between bad news for Assyria and good news for Israel. In this first chapter we encounter the proclamation that Nineveh will fall.

Chapter 2 contains incredible detail about the fall of Nineveh before it had even happened. The language of this prophecy is vivid and lively. He even describes the colour of the uniforms of the soldiers who would destroy it (red) in 2:3. This was the colour worn by the Babylonian army. Nahum also describes Assyria as a lion that will be destroyed (v.11-13) – the lion was the emblem of Assyria – and we see the lion that brought terror to all nations now being terrified (v.10). Assyria had behaved as a lion, killing its prey and bringing back enough of the plunder for its own children to live in security. Now, however, the young lions become those who are devoured by the sword (v.13).

In chapter 3, God does not judge Assyria according to the Ten Commandments but rather in terms of crimes against humanity – their barbarous cruelty. God judges people by what they know and not by what they do not know. He judges people according to that which they should instinctively know to be right as humans rather than by an external standard of which they have no knowledge. In other words, if someone has never heard of Jesus they will not be judged for rejecting him but for rejecting the knowledge of the creator that is self-evident in the world around us (Romans 1:20-21).

What happened to Nineveh after these prophecies and after its destruction? This is what Zephaniah prophesied in 2:13-15:

"He will stretch out his hand against the north and destroy Assyria, leaving Nineveh utterly desolate and dry as the desert.

Flocks and herds will lie down there, creatures of every kind. The desert owl and the screech owl will roost on her columns. Their hooting will echo through the windows, rubble will fill the doorways; the beams of cedar will be exposed.

This is the city of revelry that lived in safety. She said to herself,

"I am the one! And there is none besides me." What a ruin she has become, a lair for wild beasts! All who pass by her scoff and shake their fists."

If you go to the ancient site of Nineveh today, you will find nothing but a desert inhabited by owls with a few remains of the foundations of some of the buildings. God fulfilled the word of the prophet exactly.

The Message of Nahum

One of the questions this book answers is 'who controls history?' The book begins by reminding us of the power of Yahweh (v.3-6). 'The world trembles at his presence' and even 'the mountains quake before him'. In other words, the whole of creation is in awe at the power and majesty of the Lord. And yet within this picture we are reminded that he is 'slow to anger' (v.3), and that 'the Lord is good, a refuge in times of trouble. He cares for those who trust him' (v.7).

God has not rushed to carry out his judgement upon Assyria. He first challenged them via Jonah and now his patience has run out. It has taken 150 years for him to come to this decision. That is slow anger by anyone's measure. Why? Because the Lord always gives time for a response when he brings a word of judgement. He holds back his judgement to allow time for repentance and change. I think we can all be grateful that the Lord is not quick to anger. We try His patience all the time and yet He treats us with mercy because of His great love for us.

In 2:7, it says 'it is decreed that Nineveh be exiled and carried away'. In other words, it is God who controls history and all things will ultimately be worked out according to his plan. Humanity may think it is in control of its own destiny but ultimately it is God who will have his way on this earth.

Paul reflects this on Mars Hill in Acts 17: 26: 'From one man he made all the nations that they should inhabit the whole earth; and he marked out their appointed times in history and the boundaries of their lands'. In other words, no empire has arisen that is beyond God's control to thwart. God can destroy an empire in a very short time, just as he did the Assyrian Empire that went from world dominator to total destruction in a matter of a few years.

All of the arrogance of the rulers of the earth is built upon a false premise that they have the power to control the world. They are wrong. God is in control of this world. Even though we do not always see it, we know that nothing is beyond his power to change.

The history of the world has seen many powerful rulers arise and many dictators dominate and destroy everything in their path: Nebuchadnezzar, Cyrus, Alexander, Caesar, Attila, Genghis Khan, Napoleon, and Hitler. The list could go on. We can rest assured that each one of them will be judged just as Assyria was judged. We may not see it in our lifetime or we may not see it at all – God's judgement may not be this side of the grave – but we can be sure that it will happen because God is a God of justice and will have justice in his created order.

Paul tells us in Romans 13:1 that 'there is no authority except that which God has established'. In other words, God allows leaders to come into place as his delegated authority on the earth. Their judgement will be based on whether they have ruled justly and righteously or whether their rule has been typified by crimes against humanity. None of them will get away with it – No American or Russian president; no European leader; no Eastern potentate. They will all be brought to account by God whether they believe in him or not. This includes the leaders of every oppressive regime or terrorist group.

This knowledge should bring us some comfort. Whilst we see injustice everywhere in the world, we should do everything in our power to stand up against it (within the law). Elie Wiesel said, 'there may be times when we are powerless to prevent injustice, but there must never be a time when we fail to protest'.[4] However, we can know that, even if we do not succeed, even if the unrighteous still prevail, even if the innocent suffer, none of these leaders will get away with it forever, and God will have justice in this world.

It is also a comfort that we can look forward to that day when God sorts out all injustice. When his Son returns to the earth, he will deal with all the mess. He will bring judgement on the nations, but then he will set up his righteous reign, and there will be justice on the earth. Come Lord Jesus!

Conclusion

In this chapter, we have considered the big picture of world events, and God's hand in them, because that is where the book of Nahum has led us. However, there is a personal application that we can also consider out of this book.

Each one of us may have suffered injustice in some form. It may be bullying at school or in the work place. We may have been treated unfairly by a boss or even by a spouse. It may be as a result of a society which seems stacked against you. We all encounter injustice in some form as we move through life. The question for each one of us is how we will react as a result of it.

Our first response will probably be anger. This is understandable, but we cannot stay in anger or else it will turn to bitterness and frustration, particularly if we can do nothing to address it. At such times we need to forgive, not

---

[4]Elie Wiesel - Nobel Lecture, December 11, 1986

to let the other party off the hook, but to release ourselves from the prison of bitterness. It may be that we can take action to redress the wrong, but that is always best taken from a position of peace and not anger. It may be that we can do nothing to bring justice for ourselves but we can rest in the assurance that, when we forgive, we cease trying to get our own back and leave justice to God, knowing that he will bring about justice for every wrong committed.

Withholding forgiveness is a luxury that none of us can afford. Deal with it! If someone has hurt you or treated you badly, for your own sake forgive them. This is not a one-off action, it is a process. It starts with a decision of the will and ends in freedom. You know when you have reached that point because you can pray for and bless the one who has treated you unfairly.

Take time to deal with anger, bitterness and unforgiveness. Rest in the peace of God and trust him with the outcome. He will not fail you.

Habakkuk

Introduction

The prophecies of Habakkuk were given to Judah in the reign of Jehoiakim just prior to the invasion of the Babylonians that led to the captivity of Judah. Jehoiakim came to the throne in 608BC and the captivity occurred in 605BC, so the prophecies are given in this small window of three years.

Before the reign of Jehoiakim (and the short reign of Jehoahaz), Josiah had been king and had introduced lots of reforms. He had also reintroduced the worship of Yahweh in the Temple, restoring much that had been lost. This had been a time of revival in the land, but the two who succeeded Josiah did much to undo all of Josiah's reforms. 2 Chronicles 36:8 identifies the actions of Jehoiakim when he was king as 'detestable', and it was because of these final evils that God took away his protection away from the land, allowing it to be overrun by the Babylonians.

The name 'Habakkuk' means 'clincher'. It is a wrestling term used of one who holds onto his opponent during a bout and won't let him go. This is because, during the course of the book, Habakkuk wrestles with God concerning some very difficult questions and does not let him go until he gets some answers, similar to the manner in which Jacob wrestled with God and would not let Him go until He blessed him (Genesis 32:22-32).

Essentially, the book is split into two parts. Part 1 is in chapters 1 and 2, and Part 2 is in chapter 3. Part 1 consists of Habakkuk's question and answer session with God. Part 2 is a song of praise to God in response to all that he has heard.

Part 1

Part 1 (chapters 1-2) is made up of two questions. The first question concerns why Habakkuk observes such injustice in the land, with the wicked triumphing over the righteous, and God seems to be doing nothing about it. God's response is that he has stored up judgement for the wicked. The judgement he has in mind is the invasion of the Babylonians who will sweep through the land destroying everything (1:5-11).

This leads to Habbakuk's second question: why would God use a people as wicked as the Babylonians to execute judgement on his people who, although not living very righteously at that moment, were less wicked than the Babylonians (1:12-2:1). Habakkuk concludes this second question by saying that he is going to live on the watchtower of Jerusalem and see what God is going to do. In response, God tells him not to withdraw but to write down his prophecies on the walls and on tablets so that everyone will know about the coming judgement. He then tells him that 'the righteous person shall live by faith' (2:4). In other words, the one who is faithful and remains faithful will be preserved even in the midst of God's judgement. It is this thought that Paul picks up on when he quotes it in the New Testament (Romans 1:16-17, Galatians 3:11).

There then follows, in the remainder of chapter 2, a prophecy against Babylon saying that; despite their greed and arrogance and their use by God as an instrument of his judgement, they too will meet their comeuppance (2:4-18). In the midst of this prophecy concerning Babylon, God declares that 'the earth will be filled with the knowledge of the glory of the Lord as the waters cover the sea' (v.14). Thus, he affirms that in spite of all that is happening that seems to be so wicked, God will have his way in the earth.

The Lord concludes his response by saying:

'The Lord is in his holy temple, let all the earth be silent before him" (2:20). This is tantamount to God saying to Habakkuk 'shut up'.

Part 2

Part 2 (chapter 3) is the response of Habakkuk to the awesomeness of God. He refers to the creation as an act of God's awesomeness. He speaks of the deliverance of God's people in times past and prays that God will do it again. He stands in awe at God's deeds (v.2) and he trembles at God's might (v.16).

This whole section is unusual in that it was written to be sung. Most prophecies were poetic but were not songs, but there are indications that Habukkuk himself composed the tune for this section on his own guitar (v.19).

Habakkuk concludes with some verses that have become well known:

'Though the fig tree does not bud and there are no grapes on the vine,
Though the olive crop fails and the fields produce no food,
Though there are no sheep in the pen and no cattle in the stalls,
Yet I will rejoice in the Lord, I will be joyful in God my saviour'.

These verses sum up the meaning of this book for us. Having wrestled with God over the difficult questions that face him in an unjust and brutal world, Habakkuk concludes that, even when everything is going wrong and nothing makes sense, God is still God, and the only appropriate response is to rejoice in him as our saviour.

There are many levels on which we can consider this. As I was writing this, my thoughts kept going to what ISIS have done in the Middle East. Why has God allowed the ancient sites of Christianity to be destroyed? Why are God's people suffering such persecution and death? Why is this evil allowed to rise and take such prominence at this time? The answer is: I don't know. I do know that it is a satanically inspired evil that is bent on destroying the church that Jesus Christ laid down his life for.

There are many ways we can and should respond to crises such as these: pray, write to our MP, etc. However, I do not think we can answer the question of why God allows such things to happen. Somehow, we have to trust that, in the midst of it all, God will stand with those who suffer, that he will ultimately bring justice on the heads of those who do evil, and that he will have his will done on earth as it is done in heaven. This may not satisfy our human longing for answers, but our finite knowledge and understanding and our limited perspective cannot perceive how this will all work out. We have to trust God and pray for our brothers and sisters.

I am sure they asked similar questions in the early church as they faced first the persecutions of Nero, then Trajan and others, right the way through to Diocletian. And yet, the testimony of the early church is that, in spite of all that they faced, they remained faithful to the one who had saved them, even when faced with lions in the arena – the story of Perpetua never ceases to amaze and humble me. At the Nicene Council in 325AD, of the 318 delegates attending, fewer than 12 had not lost an eye or lost a hand or did not limp on a leg lamed by torture for their Christian faith. Let us learn from those who have gone before and trust God even when we do not have all the answers.

Another way we can consider this is in answer to the question of suffering. Many people have wrestled with this question over the centuries and I cannot pretend to be an expert on this. I could refer you to C.S. Lewis or Jurgen

Moltmann for a fuller and deeper dialogue on this question. Someone asked C.S. Lewis, "Why do the righteous suffer?" "Why not?" he replied. "They're the only ones who can take it."

However, as Habakkuk observes the innocent suffering injustice, or the wicked triumphing over the righteous, he is suitably perplexed and in search of answers.

Some say that we suffer in order for God to teach us something. Certainly, we can develop as a person in the midst of triumph and adversity, but I do not think that is the answer. God may use circumstances to get our attention, but he is not the author of suffering. John Donne suggested that the sickness which kept him in bed, forced him to think about his spiritual condition. He went on to suggest that suffering gets our attention; it forces us to look to God, when otherwise we would just as well ignore Him.[5] Thus, God may use it, as he may use all things in life, but he is not the author of our suffering – we do not suffer so that we can be taught a lesson.

To suggest this is to completely misunderstand and misrepresent the God who loves us and gave himself for us, even though he may use it if we are willing to listen.

I believe we can suffer for two reasons:

Firstly, through rebellion. If we wilfully step into rebellion, we take ourselves outside of God's protection. 'Humble yourselves, therefore, under God's mighty hand, that he may lift you up in due time. Cast all your anxiety on him because he cares for you. Be alert and of sober mind. Your enemy the devil prowls around like a roaring lion looking for someone to devour' (1 Peter 5:6-8). It is humility that keeps us under God's protection and enables us to resist the enemy. If we are in rebellion, it is open season on us. If we walk openly in

---

[5]John Donne, Hymn to God, My God, In My Sickness

rebellion against God, we cannot expect the same level of protection from him as when we are walking in righteousness.

Secondly, through living in a fallen world. Whilst Jesus came to redeem the creation, that work has not yet fully run its course. After his return, he will put all things back in order and the world will be perfect and in harmony with itself. Now, however, 'we have this treasure in jars of clay to show that this all-surpassing power is from God and not from us' (2 Corinthians 4:7). In other words, we are still frail flesh, living in a fallen world. That means that things can get broken and bad stuff can still happen. Being a Christian does not stop such things. It simply gives us the grace to endure and triumph in the midst of suffering.

This does not mean that God will not intervene in our circumstances. He will and he does. Many of us have testimonies of his protection and of his healing. We can tell stories of when God rescued us and saved us from things. And yet many of us will also have stories of when he didn't. There are no easy answers to why he may have stepped into one circumstance and not into another. The truth is, however, that 'God is good, all the time'.

The example of Paul

When I think of faith in the midst of suffering, I always come back to Paul who endured all manner of things as he sought to make the good news known. A catalogue of them is given in 2 Corinthians 11:21-29. My favourite incident, however, is the story of the storm and the shipwreck in Acts 27:21-26.

In this account, we see Paul on his way to Rome to stand before Caesar. Against Paul's advice, the ship sets out from Crete and gets caught in the most horrendous storm such that they go for 12 days and nights without seeing the sun and without eating. The ship gets tossed hither and thither on the waves and the crew are ready to despair. In the midst of the storm, Paul receives reassurance from God, and is able to impart that to the others on the ship. Despite the storm, he stands confidently trusting in God's faithfulness. Out of that, he is able to help others who are also in the midst of the storm.

When life throws its storms at us, are we the one quivering and shaking in the bottom of the boat? or are we the one who can sit in peace and confidence knowing that we have a destiny and that God is not going to let us get taken out before our time? Because Paul is living in faith in the revelation God has given regarding the future, he had no need to fear in the present, even when the storm was lashing around him. Neither do we.

God's gift to you is peace in the midst of the storm: 'Even though I walk through the darkest valley, I will fear no evil, for you are with me; your rod and your staff, they comfort me' (Psalm 23:4).

Will you trust him even when you don't understand what is happening or why evil seems to triumph in the world? Will you trust God to be God? That is the message of the book of Habakkuk.

Zephaniah

Introduction

Zephaniah was the great-grandson of King Hezekiah. He is therefore of royal blood, and perhaps knows the intrigues of the palace better than most. He was prophesying during the reign of Josiah, the reformer and last good king of Judah before the Captivity – Josiah reigned from 640BC - 609BC, and the Captivity took place in 605BC.

The mention of four generations back to Hezekiah in Zephaniah's family tree (most books only mention the father of the prophet), direct us to consider the historical run up to the prophecies of Zephaniah, especially since he was the first to prophesy in Judah since Isaiah, 70 years previously.

Isaiah had prophesied during the time of Hezekiah, but when Manasseh succeeded Hezekiah, he had Isaiah killed as he turned the nation away from the worship of Yahweh to the worship of every pagan deity.[6] The land became filled with immorality and idolatry, corruption and injustice. When Amon succeeded Manasseh, he did little to arrest the decline. When Josiah came to the throne as an 8 year old, and as he came to manhood, things began to change. Josiah introduced reforms, repaired the temple and reinstituted the worship of Yahweh. It seems that Zephaniah was one of the stimulants behind the reforms of Josiah. The name 'Zephaniah' means 'the Lord hides' or 'the Lord protects', and it may be that God protected the prophet as a child during the evil reigns of Manasseh and Amon when he was growing up.

The Message of Zephaniah

The key term in this book is 'The Day of the Lord'. It is used 23 times and is a term that signalled, not a 24-hour period,

---

[6]The Talmud [Yevamot 49b]

but a time of judgement that was coming. The judgement of which Zephaniah prophesied was on the following people in chapter 1:

- The priests who promote false worship (1:4-6)
- Officials who copy foreign customs and practice oppression (1:7-9)
- Merchants who accumulate great wealth (1:10-11)
- Sceptics who grow smug and complacent (1:12-13)

The judgement would be rapid in its approach (1:14), terrifying in its effect (1:15-16), and inescapable in its destruction (1:17-18).

In 2:1-4, the Lord gives opportunity to escape or, at least, be protected through the coming judgement. This is extended to those who humble themselves and seek him. It has ever been thus. If we want the blessing of God or the protection of God, it doesn't come through pride but through humility. It is not a right; it is a gift of God.

The prophet then goes on to proclaim that the judgement will not be limited to Judah alone but will also come upon:

- Philistia
- Moab & Amon
- Egypt and Ethiopia
- Assyria (Nineveh)

In other words, it would affect the nations to the west, east, south and north of Judah. In the years that followed, and as the Babylonians swept through the region, defeating all before them, that is exactly what did happen.

The last chapter of the book, chapter 3, returns the focus to Judah, and gives both a confirmation of the coming judgement, and a message of hope. God's promise is that he will preserve a remnant of his people (3:12), whose lips will be purified (3:9), and who will bring appropriate worship from wherever they have been scattered (3:10).

This results in singing and rejoicing by the people of God (3:14-20) as God shows once more that he is a God of restoration (3:20). It follows the period in which the punishment he sent on his people due to disobedience is now 'taken away' (3:15) because it has been exhausted.

Applying the Message of Zephaniah

As we consider the message of Zephaniah, we can see that there was an immediate application that was time bound and specific for the people of Judah at the end of the seventh century. It was a prophecy that began to be fulfilled within 15 years of being given, with the restoration being completed within 100 years of the prophecy being delivered. However, there is a part of this prophesy that is still yet to be fulfilled.

In the closing section, it is promised that 'The Lord, the king of Israel is with you; never again will you fear any harm' (3:15), and yet, we know from history that in the years following the return of Israel from captivity, the nation was first overrun and oppressed by the Greeks and then by the Romans, who brought about their scattering once more in AD70 and in AD132. In the centuries that have elapsed since then, the Jews have been further scattered across the world and oppressed in almost every place where they have lived.

But in the last 100 years, we have seen the regathering and restoring words of this prophecy starting to be fulfilled as the Jews have returned to the land, and have begun to see the restoration of all that was lost. What other nation could have survived such a scattering, and yet, because he is faithful to his promises, and despite everything that has happened to them, God has preserved a remnant of his people, and is restoring them. That work will only be complete when they recognise their Messiah as 'the Lord, the king of Israel' (3:14). At that time, national salvation will come upon Israel and the words of this prophecy will finally be fulfilled.

By New Testament times, this term, 'The day of the Lord', was loaded with meaning in the minds of those who lived in Judea and in the Diaspora. It was seen as a day in which:

- The Messiah would come
- The nations who had oppressed Israel would be judged
- The resurrection would take place
- The kingdom would come

As we know, however, some of these things were fulfilled when Jesus came, but some are deferred until he returns. Paul picks up this term in his writings and uses it specifically of the return of Jesus, and he uses it to describe all of these elements in full. He also says in 1 Thessalonians 5:2 that 'the day of the Lord will come like a thief in the night'. What does he mean by this?

He means that it will come unexpectedly to those who are not looking for it (1 Thessalonians 5:1-11). There is a clear division here between those who are living as they please, expecting the world just to get better and better towards some kind of Utopia, and those who are living as 'children of the light'.

When Paul speaks of 'peace and safety' here, these terms were part of the propaganda of the Roman Empire. The Pax Romana had brought these conditions to those who lived within its borders. In other words, Paul is saying that those who trust in political and temporal peace and security in this world will be caught unawares when it all falls apart. We need to be looking for a security beyond this temporal world system and that is tied in with the day of the Lord. Where is our security? In money, job, family, house? It needs to be rooted in God to withstand the day of trial.

There is a fantastic mixed metaphor here: We are children of the light not of the dark, so we should be sober and not drunk, awake and not sleeping and wearing our armour. What is Paul trying to say to us here?

We are not night time people who can expect judgement when the Lord returns, which will come upon those not expecting it as quickly as labour pains come upon a pregnant woman. Instead, we are daytime people. Daytime here represents the coming kingdom of the Lord, and so Paul is instructing us to live now as people of the kingdom in anticipation of the full dawning of the kingdom on the return of Jesus. That is why His coming should not surprise us – because we are living in the good of it now in expectation of its fulfilment.

Even though most of the world is still living in the night time, we need to be awake to see the dawn of God's reality upon the world. It is at night that people generally get drunk (as those of us who do Street Angels know only too well!). Drunkenness here is indicative of those who live in a way that ignores all that is coming upon the world. In other words, we cannot just live like the world lives because we know the future. Our life is a preparation for that future and so we need to be living in the good of it now. The three things that will enable us to do that are the three virtues of faith, hope and love that will be for us a helmet and a breastplate – that which protects our mind and our heart from the attack of the enemy.

Paul's message (as was Zephaniah's) is for the people of God to wake up and stop living as if the return of Jesus is not going to happen. It is nearer to us now than when we first believed. I will not make any predictions about when it will happen, whether in my lifetime or not, but I do know that it could happen very quickly and that we need to be ready and living in preparation for that day now.

How will you greet the Lord if he were to turn up today? Will it be with pleasure or shame? Will it be with rejoicing or with sorrow? I do not want to bring condemnation on anyone because we all have issues we are working on in our lives, but what we cannot do is live in complacency (Zephaniah 1:12). We need to be living with a daily expectation that the Lord will return at any moment and be seeking to see his kingdom come now, on earth, in our lives, in our families, in our town, in our nation, just as it is in heaven. That has to affect:

- Our values
- Our priorities
- Where we expend our resources (time, money, gifts)
- Which relationships we invest in
- Our behaviour

The day of the Lord is coming. Live now in the good of that fact. Be awake. Be sober. Be diligent. Rejoice at his coming.

Zephaniah 3:17

"The LORD your God is with you,
  the Mighty Warrior who saves.
He will take great delight in you;
  in his love he will no longer rebuke you,
  but will rejoice over you with singing."

God rejoices over us with singing. Let us give him something to rejoice about.

Haggai

Introduction

As we come to Haggai we move from the pre-captivity to the post-captivity period. Haggai was prophesying between 522and 516BC. It is a time of hope and restoration for the people of Israel although Haggai is prophesying into a time of discouragement for the returned exiles.

After an exile of 70 years, Cyrus the Persian emperor, in accordance with the prophecies of Isaiah and Jeremiah, had decreed that the people of Israel could return to the Promised Land to rebuild the temple in Jerusalem so that they could pray for him. A year later, some set off but, on returning to the land, they found it devastated. They built an altar and laid some foundations for the temple but, when opposition came, and, when the money from the royal purse dried up, they discontinued the work for 14 years. Instead, they set about building houses for themselves but progressed no further than that. The houses are described as 'panelled houses', i.e. panelled with wood on the inside. Since the Babylonians had chopped down all of the trees when they invaded the land, wood was a rare commodity, and so they were using their resources on building their own personal properties in a luxurious manner and had forgotten about building the house of the Lord saying, 'it's not the right time yet' (1:2).

Zerubbabel, descendent of one of the last kings of Judah, Jehoiachin, began the work of rebuilding the temple again in 520BC, in response to the prophesying of Haggai and Zechariah (see Ezra 5:1), and completed the rebuilding work in 516BC, in spite of local opposition. You can read about these events in the Book of Ezra chapters 1-6. It is against the backdrop of this rebuilding project that both Haggai and Zechariah were prophesying.

So, what did Haggai prophesy to stir up Zerubbabel to restart this work? That is what we have in the book of Haggai. It actually splits into 5 prophecies which were all given in a period of about 3 months. They concern the following:

A depressed people: 1:1-11

A determined people: 1:12-15

A discouraged people: 2:1-9

A defiled people: 2:10-19

A designated prince: 2:20-23

A depressed people: 1:1-11

Why were the people depressed? They had come back in the hope of rebuilding the nation, but it had all gone wrong, and now they were just scratching out a living with little hope for the future. They were instead concentrating on their own houses, but it seemed that, as much as they worked, it all came to nothing. Their crops were failing and the resources of the Promised Land were not sustaining them. Why was this? Surely, they should be blessed in this land, as per the promises through Abraham and Moses?

The issue for them was that their priorities were out of line and their thinking was faulty. Some of them were saying, 'it's not the right time to build the house of the Lord' (1:2), and yet that was the very purpose for which they had come back from Babylon. It was because of their disobedience to this purpose that God was not blessing them in the Promised Land.

If we want to be blessed by God, we need to put him and the building of His house as the number one priority in our lives. His criticism of these people was that they prioritised their own houses over His house. If we only concentrate on our own houses and neglect the house of God, we may benefit materially, but we will miss out on the blessing of God in our lives, and we will not fulfil our calling.

Modern values tell us that we should get a good job and get a mortgage to buy a home. We should concentrate on our children and make their concerns our number one priority, whilst increasing our material security and setting aside provision for a future. None of those things are wrong in themselves, but, if we do all of this and neglect the House of God, we rob ourselves of God's blessing, his provision, and his interaction in our lives. Hence, God, through Haggai, says to the people, 'consider your ways'. In other words, think about the way you are living and get your priorities sorted so that I can bless you.

I believe there is nothing more tragic in this world than a person with a calling from God who either gets distracted or who never lifts their game enough to fulfil it. God has placed a calling on all of our lives. It may not be something grandiose like building a temple, but he has gifted and called you for work in His house. Don't miss out on your calling. Don't miss out by being so distracted by the concerns of this life that you miss out on your destiny in God.

A determined people: 1:12-15

On hearing Haggai's words, the people responded positively and took up the challenge to begin building the house of the Lord once more. In the heart of this passage, Haggai gives them a very simple word from the Lord: 'I am with you' (1:13). Sometimes the reminder that God is with us is all we need. It is that gentle reminder by the Holy Spirit whispered into our hearts to remind us that we are never on our own and because He is with us, that brings us peace and the energy to carry on.

I believe someone reading this book needs to hear that word. God is with you. He has not left you. He will never desert you. He is alongside you.

A discouraged people: 2:1-9

After building for 27 days, some of the older members of the community were comparing the temple they were building to the temple Solomon had built which they had seen as children before the exile. In comparison, this temple was small and without much 'glory' because they had little gold or silver with which to decorate it. These comparisons were causing great discouragement amongst the people.

Into this situation, Haggai prophesied once more. First of all, the Lord reminded the leaders, Zerubbabel and Joshua (the high priest), and all the people, to 'be strong'. This is repeated three times in this passage for emphasis. In spite of all that appears to be going against them, the instruction is to be determined to carry through what they have begun. This is similar to the word of God to Joshua just before he led them into the Promised Land: 'be strong and courageous' (Joshua 1:6).

Sometimes when we face difficulties, it is steely determination, and the knowledge that we are in the purposes of God, that will pull us through and help us to overcome our discouragement.

Let's consider that word 'discouragement' for a moment. The centre part of it is 'courage'. The things that discourage us are those things that rob us of our courage or determination to complete something. When facing such things, God says to us, 'be strong, because I am with you'. This is what will encourage us and enable us to do what we are called to do.

When you are feeling discouraged be strong and know that God is with you.

There is also a second part to this prophecy where Haggai tells them that 'the glory of the latter house will be greater than the glory of the former house'. He also promises peace for Jerusalem and the wealth of nations to come to it. This is in line with the prophecies of the other prophets.

There was an immediate application to this prophecy so that, by New Testament times, with all of the Herod-funded refinements, the Temple was indeed magnificent. However, there is also a future element of this prophecy which will only be fulfilled when Israel's true glory comes into the temple, and that is Jesus himself when he returns. The writer to the Hebrews quotes these verses in 12:26-27 and tells us that the kingdom of which we are a part cannot be shaken and so, when God does shake the earth at the end of times, His Kingdom will stand.

It is his people – his living temple – that will display his glory in all the earth at that time and that will be a greater glory than any temple made with stones.

A defiled people: 2:10-19

In this section, Haggai brings the people a set of questions. The first one is, if you put dirty things with clean things, do the dirty things make the clean things dirty, or do the clean things make the dirty things clean? The answer was that the dirty things make the clean things dirty. Next, he asked them, can consecrated things make unconsecrated things consecrated? The answer, again, was no.

The message he was giving to the people was that, although they were building a consecrated thing, the temple, they themselves were unclean, indulging in some sin or other, and were in danger of defiling that which they were building. This sin is unspecified but it seems that they got the message.

Up until this point, despite them starting on the work of rebuilding the temple, they were still not experiencing God's blessing on their crops that had been withheld because of their previous disobedience about building the temple. However, once they got the message and did something about it, the response comes from heaven, 'From this day on I will bless you'.

God's desire is to bless us. This can be material or otherwise, and his desire is to enrich our lives. However, sin can hold that back. Do we want the fullness, the abundant life, that Jesus promised? Then deal with any issues of sin. All it needs is repentance – that is saying sorry and a choice of the will not to continue doing those things. It may not be immediate and it may not be easy, but as we walk these things out with God, he will bless us. If we cover them up and carry on with them, he will not. 'Consider your ways'.

A designated prince: 2:20-23

The last section is a direct word for Zerubbabel. God declares that He is in control of this world; that kings and countries only have power at His command and by His allowance. Just as this is true, so God will fulfil the calling of Zerubbabel and make him a 'signet ring' on his hand. This means that God will advance him to the position he wants him in and will reign through him.

Essentially, God was telling Zerubbabel that through him the royal line would be re-established and we know, of course, that that was fulfilled through the Messiah, Jesus. However, for Zerubbabel, this must have carried great reassurance even if he did not see it fulfilled in his lifetime.

Conclusion

In looking at this book, we are reminded to put God as our number one priority, to know that he is with us and will bless us if we align our values and priorities to his. He has a calling for each one of us to fulfil. Don't miss out on your calling through complacency or distraction. Decide from this day on that you will serve the Lord with all you are and all that you have.

Zechariah - I

Introduction

Zechariah is different to most of the other prophetic books of the Old Testament in that it was written in the post-exilic period of Israel's history, as also were Haggai and Malachi. Whereas the other prophetic books spoke into the disobedience of Israel, with proclamations of judgements and promises of restoration, the prophecies of this book were given during a time of restoration. The message of the other post-exilic books, Haggai and Malachi, were declared to stir the people out of complacency and into righteous action. Zechariah, on the other hand begins with a call to repentance to the returned exiles, but very soon moves into a set of visions and prophetic scriptures that look far beyond the immediate times in which the prophet spoke.

The name 'Zechariah' means 'God remembers', and was a common name in the Old Testament. In all there are 29 people in scripture who bear this name. He was also both a priest and a prophet.

The book begins with Zechariah reminding the people, whilst they are in the midst of rebuilding the temple, that the nation got into a mess because, despite knowing they were being disobedient to God, and despite the warnings of the prophets, they still continued in their rebellion, and bore the consequence of captivity away from the land. This was a call to repentance to the people and they responded favourably (v.6).

The Visions of the Book of Zechariah

In chapters 1 to 6 of Zechariah we have a series of eight visions. We may see these as eight parts of one vision, however, whichever way we choose to view them, there are eight distinct parts to what Zechariah sees. Since in scripture eight is the number of new beginnings, it is not surprising that these eight visions occur in Zechariah, which was given at a time of new beginning (restoration) for the people of Israel.

The visions are as follows:

1. The rider amongst the myrtle trees (1:7-17)
2. Four horns and four craftsmen (1:18-21)
3. A man with a measuring line (2:1-13)
4. Clean garments for Joshua, the High Priest (3:1-10)
5. The gold lampstand and the two olive trees (4:1-14)
6. The flying scroll (5:1-5)
7. The woman in the basket (5:5-11)
8. The four chariots (6:1-10)

We will pick out a couple of these visions to comment on.[7]

Vision 4: Clean garments for Joshua, the High Priest

In the fourth vision (3:1-10), Zechariah sees Joshua, the High Priest, standing before the Lord with Satan 'at his right hand to accuse him'. This is one of only four appearances of Satan in the Old Testament (Genesis 3, 1 Chronicles 21:1 and Job 1-2). He appears when something significant is to happen, and here he is undermining the plan of God for the priestly rulership of Israel by accusing Joshua of not being clean enough to hold the office.

Joshua is dressed in 'filthy garments' which clearly represent his uncleanness and unfitness to serve as High Priest, however, the Lord himself commands that his uncleanness be taken away and be replaced with suitable robes (v.4). Zechariah speaks up and requests that Joshua's turban is also replaced, which is done. Joshua is then instructed by the

---

[7] For a more detailed description of the content of these visions see Richard Bradbury, *It's the End of the World as we know it!* (Belvedere: Pneuma Springs, 2006), pp.99-116

Lord to walk in obedience and then his reward will be 'free access' into God's presence.

As God made provision for Joshua, so he has made provision for each one of us. Our righteousness is 'as filthy rags'. Satan has accused us and we are found wanting. However, because of what Jesus has done, we now have white robes to wear – the robes of his righteousness. Our sin is taken away and we are fit to serve in his house. He has made provision for us and given us access into his throne room.

When we serve God in any way, it must be on the basis of his righteousness not our own works. He expects us not to keep our old filthy clothes on but rather to 'clothe yourselves with compassion, kindness, humility, gentleness and patience' (Col. 3:12). He has made provision; now we must walk in it.

We are then told in verse 8 that Joshua and his friends (presumably the other priests) are a symbol, the truth of which will be demonstrated in 'the Branch'. The Branch is a term used several times in the Old Testament to indicate the Messiah (see Psalm 80:15, Isaiah 4:2, Isaiah 11:1, Jeremiah 23:5, Jeremiah 33:15). Thus, Joshua and his friends are symbols of the Messiah in his priesthood, however, it is he who will 'remove the iniquity of that land in one day' (v.9). That is exactly what he did in his sacrificial death on the cross and has thereby opened up a future of peace where 'everyone of you will invite his neighbour to sit under his vine and under his fig tree' (v.10).

Vision 5: The Gold Lampstand and the Two Olive Trees

In the fifth vision (4:1-14), after Zechariah has been roused from his sleep by an angel, he sees a golden lampstand[8] with

---

[8]For a description of the lampstand in more detail and its use in the tabernacle, see Exodus 25:31-40 and Leviticus 24:1-4. Also, note that in Solomon's temple (1 Kings 7:49), ten such lampstands were used to give light in the Holy Place, but in this rebuilt temple only one is used (see 1 Maccabees 1:21).

seven spouts and with two olive trees nearby on either side of it. In contrast with the lampstand described in Exodus 25, the lampstand in this passage has a bowl at the top. This bowl contains oil and from it oil flowed to the seven lamps[9]. From verse 12 we also know that the two olive trees pour oil from themselves and this feeds the lampstand. In observing these, he asks his angelic interpreter what the objects are, in other words, what their meaning is. The remainder of the passage is a conversation between the angel and Zechariah which defines the items.

In verse 4 Zechariah asks the angel to interpret what he is seeing. The angel expresses surprise that Zechariah doesn't already know the meaning and then goes on to explain that the vision is a symbolic representation of the word of the Lord to Zerubbabel, the governor who was responsible for the work of rebuilding the temple. The word is fourfold:

- Zerubbabel will complete the work, not in his own strength but by the anointing and enabling of the Holy Spirit (v.6). He has a continual flow of the Holy Spirit through him to complete this work. 'Not by might' indicates military strength; 'not by power' indicates political authority. In this case, Zerubbabel will complete the work through the anointing of the Holy Spirit and not through human endeavour or his role as governor.

- Zerubbabel will clear every obstacle out of the way which currently stands against the achievement of the completion of the temple (v.7).

- Zerubbabel will preside over the ceremonial fitting of the capstone, the stone that will complete the building (v.7).

- Zerubbabel laid the foundation stone of the temple and will finish the work (v.9). When this happens, this will confirm that Zechariah has indeed received the word of the Lord.

---

[9]Webb The Message of Zechariah p.91

The lampstand itself is reminiscent of Revelation chapter 1 where we see the sevenfold lampstand as representative of seven churches. In Zechariah, the lampstand represents God's people who are fulfilling His work of rebuilding the temple and will complete this work through the power of the Holy Spirit ('"Not by might, nor by power but by my Spirit" says the lord' (v.6)).

Zechariah questions further concerning the meaning of the olive trees and the angel explains in more detail concerning these (v.11-14). The angel declares that they are 'the two anointed ones who are standing by the Lord of the whole earth' (v.14). Whilst many have speculated as to whom these two might be, the obvious answer in the context of the passage is that these represent Joshua the High Priest and Zerubbabel the Governor – God's anointed and Spirit-filled leadership for the work of rebuilding the temple. Their anointing is feeding into the community as a whole and it is through the anointing on their leadership that the work on the temple will be completed.

It is no different in the kingdom of God. His kingdom will not be built by any other means than by his Spirit. We have built ecclesiastical structures and fought crusades but none of this builds the kingdom. Only the anointing of the Spirit will build that which will last. Spirit-filled anointed leadership will build the house of the Lord.

The Symbolic Crowning of Joshua the High Priest

The first half of Zechariah concludes with Zechariah being instructed by the Lord to carry out a symbolic act. He is told to take silver and gold from some who have just returned from Babylon, presumably bearing gifts for the work, and to make a crown or crowns of it. He is then to crown Joshua the High Priest and to prophesy over him. This symbolises the fact that, from this point on in Israel's history, there would no longer be a king but that the priests would guide and rule over the nation.

Zechariah is obedient, but the prophecy he gives concerns 'the branch' which is a term we know is a code word for the Messiah. Thus, Zechariah once more confirms that Joshua is a type of *Jeshua*, who will come and bear the offices of priest and king in his single personage. He will build the temple – the temple made of living stones - and He will rule.

Zechariah instructs that the crown is placed in the temple, currently under construction, as a 'memorial', i.e. a reminder to all people that the Messiah will come and fulfil this word. In this way, Zechariah concludes the first section with a continual reminder that ultimately the purposes of God concerning Jerusalem, Israel and the New Covenant people will be summed up in the coming of the Messiah.

Conclusion

The visions of the first half of Zechariah are focused on the rebuilding of the Temple in Jerusalem, but centre very specifically on Joshua, the High Priest and Zerubbabel, the Governor. These two carry political and spiritual authority in the land, and yet, for both of them, the role they are to fulfil is to be different than expected. Zerubbabel is to fulfil his work, not by means of his political leadership, but by the anointing of the Spirit. Joshua is to take on political as well as spiritual leadership in the land.

Both of these two men foreshadow the coming of Christ. He is the one who brings cleansing from sin. He is the one who combines the role of priest and king (and prophet) in his person. He is the one who achieves the building of the spiritual house of God, not through political power, but by his anointing (Messiah-ship) through the Spirit.

You and I, if we are to achieve anything for God, will not do so through 'might' or 'power' but only through the Spirit of God. The responsibility we have is to make sure we are cleansed and connected to him so that his anointing can flow in us and through us to all we meet.

Zechariah - II

Introduction

This book is specifically about God's dealings with Israel; however, since it was written in the post-exilic period, long after most of the other books of the Old Testament, its prophecies are largely centred on the coming of the Messiah, both in his incarnation, and in his glorious return. Within the oracles of chapters 9-14, it is often difficult to pick up which prophecies relate to which coming of the Lord, especially since the events prophesied are not in any particular order.

Much of the book deals with the fact that the Second Coming will be a key point of salvation for Israel and a final point of judgement upon the nations, however, the conclusion of this will be the reigning of the Messiah over Jew and Gentile alike with all participating in the worship of God and in the covenant blessings of obedience.

We cannot possibly deal with all of the materials of this section of Zechariah. We will simply pick out a few passages to focus on.

Chapters 7 to 8

In chapters 7 to 8 of Zechariah we have an interim section prior to the commencement of the prophetic oracles which take us to the end of the book. In these chapters, we see Zechariah receiving a number of specific words for the people of Israel which he delivers in prose rather than as oracles. These words act as an introduction to the prophetic oracles that follow.

In chapter 7, some people arrive from Bethel to 'seek the favour of the Lord' and to ask specifically if they can stop observing the fasts which were instituted when Jerusalem was sacked. This causes Zechariah to prophesy and to call the people as a whole to repentance, reminding them that it was due to previous disobedience that the people were driven from the land. He points out that their observance of fasting has been no different from the fasting of those against whom Isaiah prophesied in Isaiah 58, but that true fasting is accompanied with justice, kindness and compassion, not oppression and evil.

Whatever we do, whether fasting, singing, preaching, prophesying etc., if it is done without giving attention to true righteousness which includes justice and mercy, and if it is done as religious observance without substance, it is pointless. God doesn't call us to religious observance but to a faith-filled life with him. All of these things must flow out of that life and not be done for the sake of doing them. This is Zechariah's message to the men from Bethel.

Having called the people to repentance, in chapter 8 Zechariah moves on to a promise of peace, prosperity and restoration for Jerusalem. This chapter is in two parts: verses 1 to 19 relate to the immediate future of Jerusalem and verses 20 to 23 relate to a time further off. The contrast is shown by the phrase 'in these days' used in verse 15 and 'in those days' used in verse 23.

In verses 1 to 19, the prophet proclaims that the Lord 'will return to Zion and dwell in the midst of Jerusalem'. The literal translation of this is that the lord 'has' returned. Thus, the fulfilment of these words is associated with the completion of the temple (v.9), the place in which the Lord will dwell. Zechariah goes on to speak about a time of peace (v.4-5), and a further re-gathering of the scattered people of Israel (v.7-8). The lord declares that he 'will cause the remnant of this people to inherit all these things' i.e. peace and prosperity, because the purpose of the Lord is 'to do good to Jerusalem…in these days' (v.15).

Whilst these promises through Zechariah were for immediate fulfilment, they also foreshadow the condition of Jerusalem following the return of the Messiah, as detailed in the other prophetic books. Jesus came as the Prince of Peace. When he stood before Pilate he affirmed that his kingdom was not of this world and hence he was not fighting. When Pilate stood before the people, he offered them Jesus the Messiah, the Prince of Peace, or Jesus Barabbas, freedom fighter. They chose the latter and, thus, chose rebellion, not peace, and suffered the consequences in the time that followed, leading to the destruction of Jerusalem. But a time is coming when peace will return to Jerusalem, when the Prince of Peace returns in all his glory.

The final section of this chapter concerns the future.

Chapters 9 to 14 – The Prophetic Oracles

In chapters 9 to 14 of Zechariah we have a series of prophetic oracles which Zechariah delivered to the people of his day. These are not dated, as the previous visions and prophesies had been, and all concern a future time, as opposed to the time of the rebuilding of the temple.

These passages are in two oracles: the first one commences in chapter 9 and goes through to chapter 11; the second one commences in chapter 12 and concludes in chapter 14. The theme of these oracles is the coming of the king. In chapter 9, we see the first arrival of the king into Jerusalem and in chapter 14 we see the Lord as king over all. In between these depictions, we have a series of dramas presented which show us some of the events which will take place during the End Times.

Rather than dwelling on end time judgements and events, I just want to pick out the scriptures that focus on Jesus.

The First Oracle

In verses 9 and 10 of chapter 9 we see the coming of the king to Jerusalem. Clearly, this is the Messiah, who, in his coming, fulfils the earlier promises of 3:8 and 6:11-15. The confirmation that these verses deal with the coming of the Messiah is also given in the New Testament in Matthew 21:5 where the writer cites this passage to confirm the prophetic significance of Jesus' entry into Jerusalem.

Jesus fulfilled this scripture exactly as he rode into Jerusalem on a donkey. He did not turn right to go up against the Roman fort in Jerusalem; instead he turned left into the temple to drive out the corruption. He did not come to bring revolution, but to cleanse the nation. His resulting crucifixion brought cleansing to the world and unleashed the shalom peace of God to all who would come into relationship with him. This is still what he offers to those who put their trust in him.

In verse 10, we see something of the mission of the Messiah: to remove the weapons of war from Israel and to 'speak peace to the nations' as he reigns over an area that encompasses the whole world. We can interpret this in one of two ways[10]: either this is an example of prophetic foreshortening, where the first coming of the Messiah is juxtaposed with the outcome of the Second Coming (the reign of the Messiah over all the earth), or we can take it that Christ now reigns over all the earth, and that his mission was to bring peace to the nations – peace with God. It is certainly true that all things are subjected to Him now (Ephesians 1:22), and, in that sense, this prophecy has already been fulfilled, however, on His return, His enemies will be made His 'footstool' (Hebrews 1:13, 10:13).

---

[10]Interpretation of this verse is dependent on the millennial view taken by the reader (see Richard Bradbury, *It's the End of the World as we know it!*).

The 'peace' here promised on the coming of the Messiah is 'shalom' peace which means 'wholeness and well-being'. This is only available through the presence of Jesus with us.

In 9:11-17, the final victory of the Messiah is foreseen but particularly from the perspective of Israel. The passage starts with the words 'as for you' referring to those who are associated with him because of the blood covenant with them. The Lord goes on to declare the restoration of 'double' to them and his use of them 'as my bow' (v.13) in 'saving them in that day' (v.16). It is clear that following this 'day' will come a time of peace and prosperity upon the land and its inhabitants.

These themes are picked up again in chapter 10. In this chapter we have the restoration of Israel to the land, ('I will whistle for them to gather them together for I have redeemed them', v.8, see also v.6, 9-10), and also his use of them to go against his / their enemies (v.3-5). As part of the re-gathering, the enemies will be defeated (v.11). It is declared that much of the situation Israel finds itself in is because of poor shepherding (v.2-3), which causes God's anger to rise, but which results in him bringing about the restoration and salvation of his people himself.

In chapter 11, the theme of the shepherding of God's people is picked up once again. In this chapter, we see that the shepherd's 'glory is ruined' (v.3). In other words, all that the leaders have been leading is destroyed. This is then followed by two parables acted out by Zechariah which summarise God's dealing with his people.

Together, these parables show that God's desire to shepherd his people has been rejected, and the consequence of such rejection will always result in foolish shepherds being raised up, and in the people being handed over to the oppressors. This has already been demonstrated in Israel's history, and has continued to be the case following Zechariah's day, through the inter-testamental period, when Israel was the buffer zone for the wars between the Ptolemaic and Seleucian dynasties, right through to the dispersion in AD 70. The hope for Israel in this respect is their ultimate acceptance of their Messiah, and this has already been promised in chapters 9 and 10.

Within the midst of this prophecy, in 11:12-13, we see the purchase price for Jesus affirmed: 30 pieces of silver.

The Second Oracle

The second oracle is contained in chapters 12 to 14.

At the start of chapter 12 we jump straight away to the End Times with the nations surrounding Jerusalem and with God using Jerusalem as 'a cup that causes reeling' (or 'to stagger as though drunk'). We are told that 'all the nations of the earth will be gathered against it' (v.3), but God will fight on their behalf (v.4), and ultimately will 'set about to destroy all the nations that come against Jerusalem' (v.9).

In verse 10, we see the repentance of the people of Israel as they look upon Jesus 'whom they have pierced' (the piercing suggested here is a stabbing which is a death blow) as he comes as their king to deliver them. They will not only recognise that he has previously been pierced, but that they were the ones responsible for it. It is at this point that they will acknowledge him and 'mourn...as one mourns for an only son'. What is described here is the mourning and contrition of the whole nation, individually and collectively (v.11-14). This is what Paul affirms in Romans 9-11, resulting in the salvation of the whole nation. The mourning is as a result of the fact that they have wasted 2,000+ years in not recognising him.

David Pawson suggests that all it takes for a Jew to accept Jesus as his Messiah is to know that he is alive[11]. On that day in the future, the whole nation will see him and recognise the wounds upon him and turn en masse to accept his salvation.

In chapter 13 we move from mourning to cleansing as God, himself, opens up a fountain for the inhabitants of the land to come 'for sin and for impurity' (v.1). The consequence of the mourning is that the grace of God is poured out upon his people, and this results in repentance, leading to a cleansing of the land from idols, false prophets (v.2-6) and 'the unclean spirit from the land' (v.3).

Chapter 13 concludes with a short poem in which, in verse 7, God's shepherd is struck and his sheep scattered. Jesus himself declared in Matthew 26:13 that the fulfilment of this scripture was in his own death on the cross which resulted in his disciples being scattered, however, the consequence of his death (his rejection by his people) was the dispersion of the whole of Israel and that is also prefigured here. The poem then jumps to the final day with which chapter 12 began and declares that, at that time, the time of the last battle against the nations, two thirds of Israel will 'perish' (v.8), and the remaining third will be refined 'through the fire'. It is at that point that they will call on his name and be delivered, redeemed and restored to relationship with God saying, 'the Lord is My God' (v.9).

This brings us to chapter 14 which is in two parts. The first part (verses 1 to 8) give us a very clear picture of the events which will unfold on the day the Lord returns to Jerusalem as its Messiah and Saviour; in verses 9-21, Zechariah opens up something of the world as it will be during the reign of the Messiah on earth.

---

[11] Pawson, *Unlocking the Bible*, (p.751)

The events leading up to the coming of the Lord portray a time of great struggle for the people of Israel, and particularly for those living in Jerusalem at that time. We are told in verse 2 that 'the nations will be gathered' against Jerusalem. This is a reiteration of 12:2-3. We are also told that the city will be taken and half of the inhabitants exiled (v.2). It is at that point, when Israel appears to be on the point of capitulation, that 'the Lord will go forth and fight against those nations' (v.3). He will come to the Mount of Olives (c.f. Acts 1:11,) and as he stands on it, it will be split in two creating a valley of escape for the remaining inhabitants of the city (v.5-6). At this point we are told that with his coming he will have 'the holy ones with him'. This is confirmed in 1 Thessalonians 4:14: 'even so, God will bring with him those who have fallen asleep in Jesus'.

In verses 9-21, Zechariah opens up various aspects of the post-second coming world. He starts by stating that 'the Lord will be king over all the earth' (v.9). At this point we reach the climax of human history, when the rulership of the world, which was originally given to man who, through his sin, passed it on to Satan, is returned into the hands of God. The history of the world from beginning to end will have come full circle, and, at that time, God, in the form of a man, will reign over all the earth, fulfilling the Divine mandate given to the first humans.

In verse 16, the scene changes to dealing with the remnant of the nations who will be required, with the people of God, to come up to Jerusalem annually to celebrate the Feast of Tabernacles. This feast was a celebration of God's goodness at the time of harvest, commemorating the Israelite's journey in tents through the wilderness. It is fitting that, during this time, the world is still called to celebrate God's goodness and provision and the completion of the journey into the Kingdom of God. However, it is clear that, whilst this celebration is expected, the peoples of the earth are not coerced into celebrating it, although the consequences of them not doing so are the removal of God's blessing from their lands and a plague that will come upon them. This tells us that the world in this period will not be perfect and that the nations may still be rebellious, however, the consequences of such rebellion will be direct and tangible, since the Lord himself will be present on earth.

The chapter, and the book, conclude by affirming that just about everything in Israel, including the cooking pots, will be declared 'HOLY TO THE LORD'.

Conclusion

As we conclude this whistle-stop tour of Zechariah, I want to finish by saying that, just as the prophecies concerning the first coming of the Messiah contained within this book were fulfilled so accurately, so will those concerning his Second Coming be fulfilled.

We can look forward to that day with confidence knowing that our redeemer is coming and will put the world right.

Malachi

Introduction

We come now to the last of the minor prophets, Malachi. This book is not only the last book in the Old Testament, it is also the last book of the canon written, and is dated about 100 years after Zechariah (about 20 years after Nehemiah rebuilt the walls). The word 'Malachi' simply means 'messenger', thus, Malachi is not the name of the prophet who delivered these prophecies. Rather they are delivered by an anonymous prophet as God's last word to his Old Testament people.

The situation is that the temple has been up and running for a while, and more people have gradually returned to the land. However, they are still not living as they should according to the covenant. In fact, the society had become plagued with injustice. The people had become apathetic in following the law and in worship of God. They were lax and complacent in terms of their morals. They were going through the motions of practicing their religion.

This book highlights a number of areas where this is so, before telling them to prepare for the coming Messiah, 'the great and terrible day of the Lord'. The prophet begins by highlighting the shortcomings of the priests and then goes on to identify those of the people.

The Priests

For the priests, there are two essential areas where they are falling short. The first one is in offering cheap sacrifices and thinking they will be acceptable (v.6-8). Instead of offering animals that were without blemish, they were offering the blind, lame and diseased animals. In other words, they were offering cut-price sacrifices.

Malachi tells them that they would not offer the governor a cut-price animal as an offering and yet they think it is ok to offer that to God.

How about us? Does God get the best of us, or the bit that's left over when we have satisfied ourselves in every way? Does he get the first honour in the mornings or our thoughts and prayers during the day, or only when we need something from him? Does he get worship on a Sunday or only if we do not have a better offer?

All of this dishonours him. It speaks of where our heart is really at. The Lord says to them that they would be better shutting up the temple and not offering any more sacrifices than to offer them half-heartedly. In the same way, if we as a people are not giving ourselves totally to God in our lives and worship, we might as well close our churches and go and do something else instead. God hates half-heartedness. He would rather we are either hot or cold than half-hearted.

The second thing the Lord corrects the priests about is that they are not preaching the truth, and are, therefore, causing the people to stumble (2:7-8). The responsibility of those who teach the Word of God is to bring people into the truth. It is not to tickle people's ears or to tell people what they want to hear. It is to take this book and present it in such a way that people will both understand it and live it.

There are too many preachers out there who build up popularity around entertaining people or giving people a few nice thoughts. Such preachers sell the people of God short. The Word imparts life and the truth sets people free.

I am not here to entertain or to make people feel good (although that may result from the Word). I am here to impart truth in order to equip the people of God to fulfil their calling and to live more godly lives. It may not always be popular. It may not always be comfortable, but if I do otherwise, I sell you short.

You don't have to look far to see people who have built huge ministries by entertaining people. But the Truth is too important to water down, to popularise or to make blunt. It is a 'two-edged sword able to separate soul and spirit, bone and marrow' (Hebrews 4:12).

The People

Having dealt with the priests, Malachi then turns his attention on the people. He picks up on five areas where they were failing:

- Mixed marriages
- Heartless divorce
- Doubtful questions
- Unpaid tithes
- Slanderous Talk

We'll take each of these in turn.

Mixed Marriages

According to 2:11-12, the issue for Israel was that they were to keep themselves pure as a nation, and only marry from within the tribes. Instead, for whatever reason, they had started to intermarry with people from the surrounding nations. Nehemiah had challenged them concerning this twenty years earlier (Nehemiah 13:23-27), and yet they had continued to do it. Why was this such an issue? Because the foreign partners brought with them their foreign gods and thus the children would easily be led into idolatry again.

I believe Christians, too, should not intermarry. I am not talking about race here but a Christian should not marry a non-Christian. When a Christian marries a non-Christian this is like an unequal yoke and two cannot walk together unless they are agreed. In my life I have seen so many people ship-wreck their faiths or struggle in their marriage by not adhering to this practice. When they are young and in love they say, 'but he allows me to practice my faith', or 'I am believing that she will come to faith'. But the reality is that it never (or rarely) happens. Instead it becomes a source of conflict and compromise.

When our heart is set on following God, how can we possibly marry someone who disregards him? Don't do it. It will end in tears. If you are in relationship with someone now and you are beginning to have deep feelings for them, but they are not a Christian, end it now before you get in too deep. This may seem harsh, but please learn from those who have gone before you.

Heartless Divorce

The next issue for these people was heartless divorce (2:13-16). The people had moved into a place where, when their wives got too old, and they were no longer so attractive, they were trading them in for a younger model. The issue was not divorce per se, but the heartless manner in which they were moving from one spouse to another.

God accuses them of being 'unfaithful to the wife of their youth'. God's ideal is always that we remain faithful to one another as that is a picture of our faithfulness to him. However, in this case, the people were ignoring such an ideal. Their attitude towards their wives was similar to their attitude towards God. As long as she served his needs, he would keep her, but when he grew tired of her, or fancied someone else, he would depart from her.

In the same way, they had a come-day go-day attitude towards God. As long as he was blessing them, they would be faithful, but if they weren't seeing the blessing, then they would not be so diligent. However, they failed to see that they were not seeing the blessing because they were not being diligent or consistent in the way they were living.

For each one of us, God calls us to be faithful to him. For those of us who came to faith many years ago, some of us in our childhood, we were excited and enthusiastic. But as the years have gone on our enthusiasm has dulled and we have lost the first love with which we entered into that faith. God's call on us is to stop flirting with everything else in life that attracts us, and put him as number one again.

In our lives many things vie for our attention: work, money, sport, job, etc. None of these things are wrong in themselves, but do not let them replace God in your affections. Do not be unfaithful to the Lord.

Doubtful Questions

In 2:17, we catch a glimpse of what was going on in the minds of Israel at that time. They were saying untruths about God and his dealings with them, which were reflecting their attitudes. On the one hand they were saying that it does not matter how you live and how you behave, God will still bless you. On the other hand, they were saying that God is not just in his dealings with people.

We hear both of these attitudes all around us all of the time. People live expecting to be blessed because God is a God of love, without any regard for behaviour or lifestyle. Despite disregarding God and his word, they then turn around and blame God for everything that goes wrong.

I cannot guarantee that if you do what's right, life will be easy. I can guarantee, however, that if you live as God wants you to live, you will experience his blessing in your life. It may not be material or financial blessing, but he will be with you no matter what life throws at you.

Unpaid Tithes

Next we come to the thorny issue of tithing (3:6-12). For Israel, tithing was covenantal. That is, as part of the agreement between themselves and God that would guarantee his material blessing upon them, they were to give 10% of their income, their crops, etc. back to God. This was to be used to ensure that the Levites had enough to live on to enable them to perform their temple and other duties.

In the New Covenant, we are not bound to tithing as a means to secure our blessing from God. That is why tithing is not taught anywhere in the New Testament. Rather, we are encouraged to give with a cheerful heart. 2 Corinthians 9:7 says

'Let every man give according to the purposes in his heart, not grudgingly or out of necessity, for God loves a cheerful giver.'

We are not called to give 10% but to give everything we have and everything we are back to God. Out of all that he gives us as stewards of his resources, he then asks us to consider carefully what is appropriate and right to give.

Just as the tithe was used to support the work of the Levites, so our giving should be used to support the work of ministry. Paul is very clear about this in the above passage and also in 1 Corinthians 9. Also, just as Israel were told to 'bring the whole tithe into the storehouse,' so I believe the local church is the storehouse into which we should be giving.

Should we give 10% of our earnings? I believe this is a good starting point, but Paul makes it very clear that our giving should flow out of our heart and not out of legalism. The key here is that we should be giving generously to ensure the work God has given us to do in our location can go forward.

Slanderous Talk

In 3:14-15, they were slandering God by saying that it was a waste of time serving him because they never get anything out of it. This is never a good thing to do.

This all smacks of arrogance. We must never forget that God owes us nothing and has given us everything. We are blessed beyond measure, and it is our privilege to serve him, and to be in relationship with him, not just for what we can get out of it.

The Day of the Lord

Amongst all of these challenging words, God also makes some promises to the people.

In 3:1-6, God promises that he will send his 'messenger' (his Malachi) to them who will sort everything out. He will refine them and deal with all of the evil and injustice in the land. In this passage is a promise of the first coming of Jesus, when he came to the temple (v.1) to refine it of corruption. But it also looks forward to his Second Coming when he will refine the land once and for all.

The book concludes with a reminder of the Law Moses gave them (4:4) and the promise that Elijah will come to them before the coming of the Lord.

This Elijah coming was fulfilled in John the Baptist. He wore the same clothes as Elijah (2 Kings1:8); he ate the same food as Elijah; he proclaimed a message of repentance the same as Elijah did; he also died the death planned for Elijah by Jezebel – a death by the edge of the sword by a wicked queen.

Thus, the book (and the Old Testament) concludes with a promise, but also with a warning. It draws upon the other scriptures to remind us that the day of the Lord will also be terrible for some, 'but for you who revere my name, the sun of righteousness will rise with healing in its rays' (4:2).

Conclusion

As we have journeyed through the Minor Prophets, we have entered the world of the past, and we have seen that little has changed. People encountered the same encouragements and disappointments that we face. The world was a turbulent place, just as it is now. In the midst of this, people continued with their lives, sometimes walking with God, and, at other times, walking away from him.

The prophets did not have an easy time of it. Some were killed and others rejected, and yet, within each one of them, was the need to make known the revelation God had given to them for their nation or for the nations around them. Some of these words gave reassurance and hope; some brought challenge and confrontation; some brought predictions of outright judgement. These men did not hold back (with the exception of Jonah) from delivering that which God had given them, regardless of the consequences.

For us, whatever role God has called us to play, we can learn from the steely obedience of these men. The journey God would take us on is not always easy and will sometimes result in the rejection of those around us, but obedience to God is far more important than the acceptance of humanity, and will reap an eternal reward.

The underlying message of all of these books is that God expects obedience from his people – that is the place of blessing. The onus is on us to lay aside all that distracts us and seek to follow Him in all our ways.

God bless.

Bibliography

Bradbury, Richard, *It's the End of the World as we know it!* (Belvedere: Pneuma Springs, 2006)

Donne, John, *Hymn to God, My God, In My Sickness*

Oasis, *Whatever*, 1994

Pawson, David, *Unlocking the Bible: A Unique overview of the whole Bible* (London: Harper Collins, 2007)

Prior, David, *The message of Joel, Micah & Habakkuk*, (Leicester: IVP, 1988)

Talmud, The, [Yevamot 49b]

Wiesel, Elie, Nobel Lecture, December 11, 1986

About Richard Bradbury

Leading a church in Yorkshire and travelling to teach in India and Africa, Richard Bradbury's books arise out of the experience of 30 years of church leadership. Aiming to bring the truth of the Word of God to the wider Body of Christ, Richard writes in a no-nonsense, informed fashion approaching difficult doctrine head on with the aim of bringing clarity to the understanding of his readership. Married with four children and with a background in management alongside church leadership, Richard brings the benefit of the skills honed in all of these arenas to bear in his writing.

Book(s) by Richard Bradbury

It's the End of the World as we know it (ISBN: 9780954551063)
This book has been written as a 'users guide' to the end times so that the reader can understand from the Bible the events leading up to the return of Christ in order that they may, when they 'see all these things, recognise that He is near, right at the door'.

Losing My Religion - The Radical Message of the Kingdom (ISBN: 9781907728174)
The Kingdom of God is the most important and fundamental doctrine in the Christian faith; everything else hangs off this truth and, unless we grasp this, we will miss the whole point of our faith. The hope of the author is that the reader will get hold of this same understanding and apply its implications to their own world.

Everybody Hurts - A Foray into the Minor Prophets (ISBN: 9781782284406)
The minor prophets are often neglected and rarely preached on. Perhaps we are frightened of prophetic texts or find them inaccessible, or perhaps we just can't see what relevance the 2000-year-old rantings of a bunch of dead men have in the 21st Century world. Journey through this book and see a present-day application, relevant for your life today.

Lightning Source UK Ltd.
Milton Keynes UK
UKOW06f0040171117
312863UK00001B/12/P